Better Homes and Gardens®

WOOD™

KIDS' PROJECTS

YOU CAN MAKE

WE CARE!

All of us at Meredith® Books are dedicated to giving you the
information and ideas you need to create beautiful and useful
woodworking projects. We guarantee your satisfaction with this
book for as long as you own it. We also welcome your comments
and suggestions. Please write us at Meredith® Books, BB-117,
1100 Walnut St., Des Moines, IA 50309-3400.

A WOOD™ BOOK
Published by Meredith® Books

MEREDITH® BOOKS
President, Book Group: Joseph J. Ward
Vice President and Editorial Director: Elizabeth P. Rice
Executive Editor: Connie Schrader
Art Director: Ernest Shelton
Prepress Production Manager: Randall Yontz

WOOD® MAGAZINE
President, Magazine Group: William T. Kerr
Editor: Larry Clayton

KIDS' PROJECTS YOU CAN MAKE
Produced by Roundtable Press, Inc.
Directors: Susan E. Meyer, Marsha Melnick
Senior Editor: Sue Heinemann
Managing Editor: Ross L. Horowitz
Graphic Designer: Jeff Fitschen
Design Assistant: Leslie Goldman
Art Assistant: Ahmad Mallah
Copy Assistant: Amy Handy

For Meredith® Books
Editorial Project Manager/Assistant Art Director: Tom Wegner
Contributing How-To Editors: Marlen Kemmet,
    Charles E. Sommers
Contributing Tool Editor: Larry Johnston
Contributing Outline Editor: David A. Kirchner

Special thanks to Khristy Benoit

On the front cover: Fun-Time Tote Box, pages 79-81
On the back cover: Kids' Play Structure, pages 5-10;
    Wall-Hung Game Cabinet, pages 38-41, One Lean Jelly
    Bean Machine, pages 76-78

FOR THE
GREAT OUTDOORS

Make it easy for youngsters to have fun outdoors with these projects for different play structures, a picnic table, a wagon, and sports equipment, including a baseball bat.

KIDS' PLAY STRUCTURE

School will soon be out, and wouldn't it be great to turn your youngsters or grandchildren loose with this versatile play structure this summer? We guarantee they won't want to leave the backyard.

Kids can swing from the rear extension, operate the boom out front, or simply hide away in the platform clubhouse. The sturdy construction rests on four treated 4x4 posts anchored in concrete in the ground.

The play center pictured here took a team of two about three weekends to complete. Cost for materials in our town was approximately $500.

If you wish, simplify the design by eliminating the crane and swing. Presto! You have a "treeless" tree house or an Army blockhouse.

One caution, though: You'll probably get the urge to climb in and play awhile yourself. It's OK—we're all kids at heart!

Note: We designed this structure for children 5 years and older. Safety bars in the round windows and in the roof "lookout tower" help restrict access to the roof. You can't be too safe when it comes to kids! Also, we divided the Bill of Materials into three sections to keep the items with the drawing where the parts are shown. The supplies for the entire play structure appear on page 8.

Phase I:
Setting the posts

1. From 4x4 pressure-treated stock, cut two each of parts A, B, and C to length, as indicated in the Post Layout drawing at *right*. Mark and bore the ⅞" holes ¾" deep in A, B, and C where shown in the

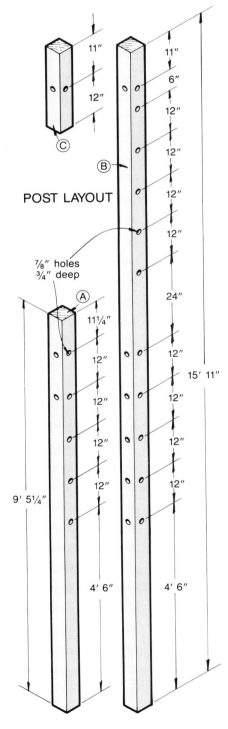

POST LAYOUT

drawing. (Remember that you are working in pairs of A's, B's, and C's, and that the holes in one A must be a mirror image of those in the other.) Mark all the hole locations in each pair first to ensure that you drill along the correct edges of each post. Set the short 4x4s (C) aside for now; you'll use them later when building the roof. Cut the ¾" conduit rungs (D) to length with a hacksaw.

Note: We set the posts of our play structure 42" deep in concrete for stability and protection from frost heaving. You may need to set the posts even deeper in the northern-most areas of the country. If you go deeper, remember to cut the posts longer initially to keep the structure at the same height above ground as shown.

2. Lay out the location of the four postholes. They should measure 20½" from center to center. Using a posthole digger, dig four 8"-diameter holes at least 12" deep.

3. Insert the conduit rungs (D) between the tall posts (B), using pipe clamps to help force the rungs into the holes. With a helper, stand the assembly up and slide it into the holes, with the tall posts positioned at the end you want the boom of the crane to point. Put the short posts in the holes and finish installing the rungs.

4. *Important:* Checking that the posts are plumb in both directions and that the rungs are level, brace the posts as shown in the sketch on the bottom of this page. Mix and pour concrete into the holes.

Building the support structure

1. Let the concrete cure for 24 hours before further work is performed on the structure. Meanwhile cut the joists (E), header joists (F), and headers (G) to length, as indicated in the Bill of Materials on *page 6.*

Safety Note: *Much of the assembly now takes place several feet off the ground. You need a sturdy stepladder, extension ladder, and a helper for safety's sake.*

2. Level and clamp two joists (E) to the four posts where shown in the Construction Phase I drawing.
continued

KIDS' PLAY STRUCTURE
continued

Bill of Materials

	FOR PHASE I OF CONSTRUCTION				
Part	Finished Size			Mat.	Qty.
	T	W	L		
A	3½"	3½"	9' 5¼"	4X4 (treated)	2
B	3½"	3½"	15' 11"	4X4 (treated)	2
C	3½"	3½"	1' 11"	4X4 (treated)	2
D	¾"	(⅞" O.D.)	18½"	conduit	26
E	1½"	5½"	4' 9"	2X6 (treated)	4
F	1½"	5½"	5' 0"	2X6 (treated)	2
G	1½"	5½"	1' 5"	2X6 (treated)	2
H	¾"	1' 8¾"	5' 0"	ext. plywood	1
I	¾"	3' 3¼"	5' 0"	ext. plywood	1
J	¾"	1' 6¼"	2' 1¼"	ext. plywood	1

CONSTRUCTION PHASE I

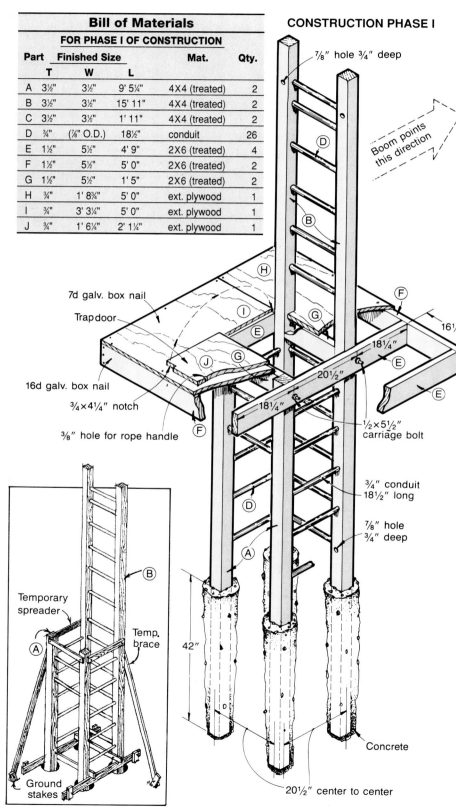

7d galv. box nail

Trapdoor

16d galv. box nail

¾×4¼" notch

⅜" hole for rope handle

Temporary spreader

Temp. brace

Ground stakes

⅞" hole ¾" deep

Boom points this direction

16½"

18¼"

20½"

18¼"

½×5½" carriage bolt

¾" conduit 18½" long

⅞" hole ¾" deep

42"

20½" center to center

Concrete

Then drill the holes and bolt both E's to the posts. Complete the platform framing by nailing in place the headers (G), the header joists (F), and finally the outside joists (E) where shown in the drawing.

3. Cut the platform-flooring panels (H, I) to size from ¾" treated exterior plywood. Nail the flooring to the joists and headers, trimming if necessary to keep the edges of the flooring panels flush with the edges of the joists and headers. Note that part H needs to be notched and that it covers only half of header G, leaving a recess for the trapdoor to close flush. When cutting the trapdoor hole in part I, line up the three cuts with the centers of the joists (E) and header (G). Making straight cuts will allow you to use the cutout in part I as the trapdoor (J). Notch the corners of the trapdoor where shown.

4. Mount the trapdoor to I with two 3" strap hinges. Drill a ⅜" hole through the door. Run a piece of rope through the hole and tie a knot on the bottom, then loop the top of the rope and secure it with a knot to form a handle for the door.

Phase II:
Erecting the frame

1. Cut the studs (K) and top plates (L, M), side window headers (N), window safety bars (O), and boom window headers and sills (P) to length. Drill ¾" holes ¾" deep in the studs (K) for the window bars, where shown in the Side Section drawing. Drill holes in two K's for the safety bars to prevent access through the swing-support opening.

2. Toenail the studs (K) to the floor (you'll need to use some temporary braces until you nail the top plates in place). Install the window bars between the window studs, where shown in the side and rear openings. Nail the top plates and window headers in position, using pipe clamps to hold the

CONSTRUCTION PHASE II

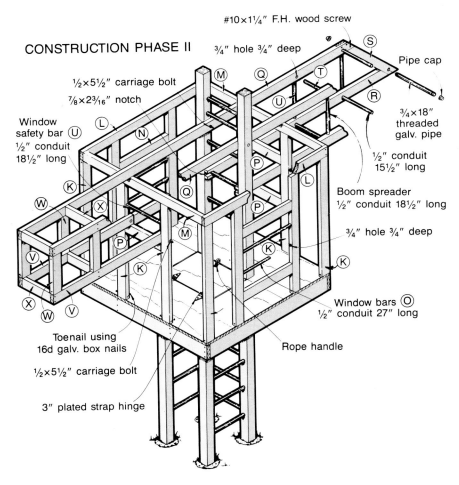

#10×1¼" F.H. wood screw

¾" hole ¾" deep

Pipe cap

½×5½" carriage bolt

⅞×2³⁄₁₆" notch

¾×18" threaded galv. pipe

Window safety bar Ⓤ
½" conduit 18½" long

½" conduit 15½" long

Boom spreader
½" conduit 18½" long

¾" hole ¾" deep

Window bars Ⓞ
½" conduit 27" long

Toenail using 16d galv. box nails

Rope handle

½×5½" carriage bolt

3" plated strap hinge

headers and window bars in position. (The framework will still be a bit wobbly at this point, but not to worry—the rest of the framework and plywood will stabilize it.)

Building the boom

1. Cut the upper arms (Q), lower arms (R), arm ends (S), and conduit boom spreaders (T, U) to size. Miter-cut and form a 45° mitered half lap on *one* end of each Q and R, and *both* ends of each S, where shown in the Side Section drawing on *page 8* and the Construction Phase II drawing *above*. (We mitered the ends of our pieces with a miter saw. Then we mounted a dado blade in the radial-arm saw, set the miter angle at 45° and cut the half-lap joints.)

2. Lay out and drill ¾" holes ¾" deep in each Q and R. See the

Side Section drawing for locations. These holes will accept T and U.

3. Measure 6' 1¼" from the mitered end of each upper arm (Q), and drill a hole through the center of each arm and through the two taller posts (B). Using ½×5½" carriage bolts, bolt the upper arms to the B posts. Clamp the upper arms to the top plates (M) so that the distance between the arms is constant from end to end. Then nail the arms to the top plates.

4. Notch the lower arms (R) to fit around one of the conduit rungs inside the structure. Install the boom spreaders. Assemble the mitered end of the boom using epoxy and four #10×1¼" F.H. wood screws per joint where shown in the Construction Phase II drawing. [Be sure to allow room for the 1⅛" pipe holes that you will drill later in the end of the lower boom joints (R, S).]

5. Using an expansion bit, drill 1¹⁄₁₆" holes in the ends of the lower boom joints (R, S) where shown in the Construction Phase II drawing. Cut ¾" galvanized pipe to length, and have both ends threaded (most hardware or plumbing supply stores will thread pipe for a small charge). Install the pipe in the holes in both lower booms and attach the pipe caps. (We used epoxy on the threads to prevent the caps from unthreading.)

6. Bolt the lower boom arms (R) to the appropriate studs (K).

Phase III:
Building the swing support and rafter assembly

1. Cut the two lower swing arms (V) and swing-arm supports (W, X) to size. Nail the pieces together, where shown in the Construction Phase II drawing. Nail to the upper arms (Q) and bolt the lower supports (V) to the studs (K).

2. Cut the top and bottom plywood panels (Y) to size. With construction adhesive and nails, fasten them to the swing support assembly, where shown in the Construction Phase III drawing on *page 9*. Drill and install two 6" eyebolts to support the swing. (We

continued

Bill of Materials				
FOR PHASE II OF CONSTRUCTION				
Part	Finished Size		Mat.	Qty.
	T	**W**	**L**		
K	1½"	3½"	4' 2¼"	2X4 (treated)	12
L	1½"	3½"	5' 0"	2X4 (treated)	2
M	1½"	3½"	4' 9"	2X4 (treated)	2
N	1½"	3½"	2' 0"	2X4 (treated)	4
O	½" dia. (⅞" O.D.)		2' 1½"	conduit	4
P	1½"	3½"	1' 5"	2X4 (treated)	3
Q	1½"	3½"	13' 6"	2X4 (treated)	2
R	1½"	3½"	8' 0"	2X4 (treated)	2
S	1½"	3½"	3' 1"	2X4 (treated)	2
T	½" dia. (¾" O.D.)		1' 3½"	conduit	4
U	½" dia. (¾" O.D.)		1' 6½"	conduit	5
V	1½"	3½"	4' 1½"	2X4 (treated)	2
W	1½"	3½"	1' 5"	2X4 (treated)	4
X	1½"	3½"	1' 2"	2X4 (treated)	4
Y	¾"	1' 5"	1' 11⅜"	ext. plywood	2

KIDS' PLAY STRUCTURE

continued

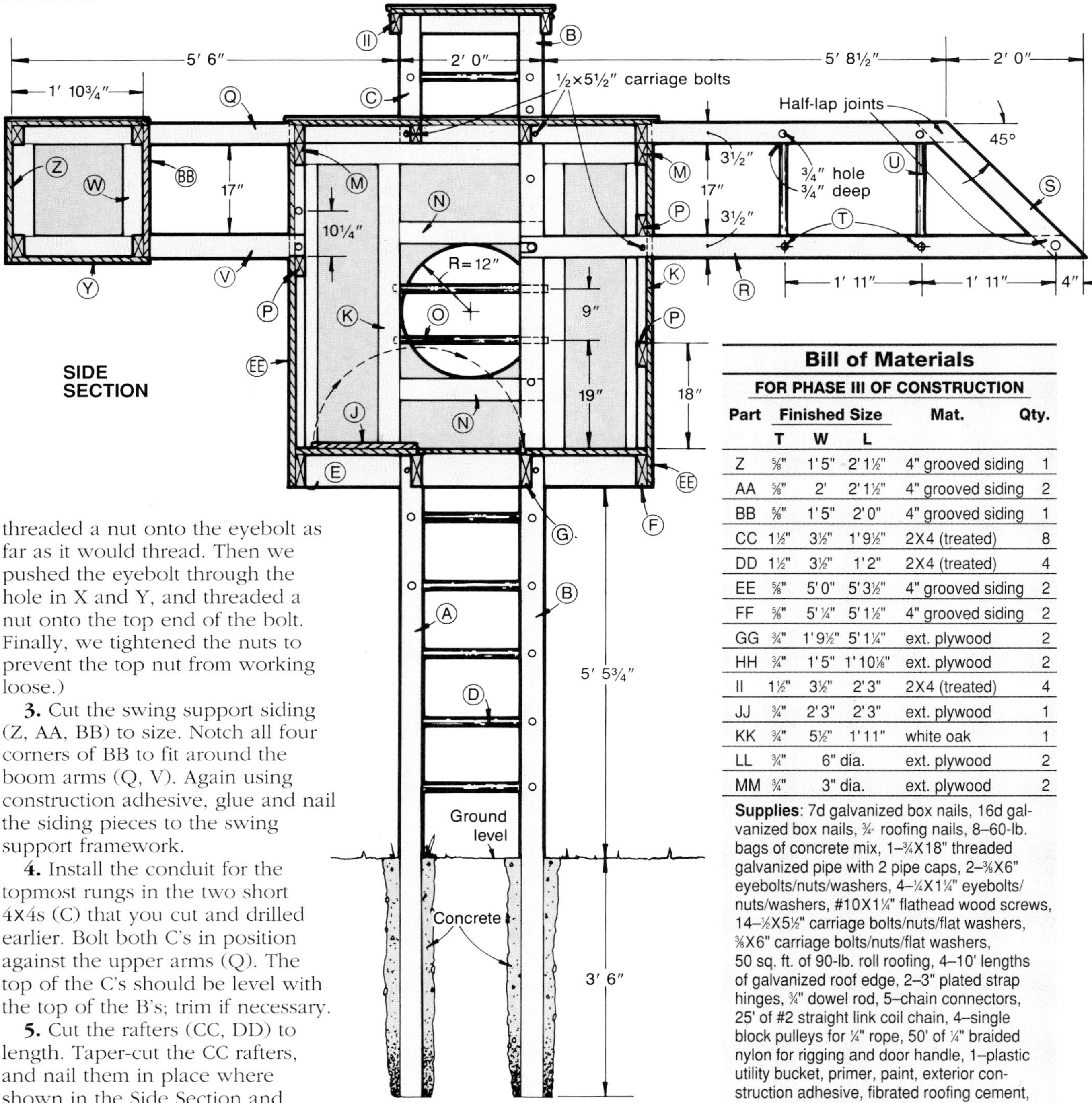

SIDE SECTION
5′ 6″
1′ 10¾″
2′ 0″
5′ 8½″
2′ 0″
½×5½″ carriage bolts
Half-lap joints
45°
17″
3½″
3½″
¾″ hole
¾″ deep
10¼″
R=12″
9″
19″
18″
1′ 11″
1′ 11″
4″
5′ 5¾″
3′ 6″
Ground level
Concrete
A
B
C
D
E
F
G
J
K
M
N
O
P
Q
R
S
T
U
V
W
Y
Z
BB
EE
II

threaded a nut onto the eyebolt as far as it would thread. Then we pushed the eyebolt through the hole in X and Y, and threaded a nut onto the top end of the bolt. Finally, we tightened the nuts to prevent the top nut from working loose.)

3. Cut the swing support siding (Z, AA, BB) to size. Notch all four corners of BB to fit around the boom arms (Q, V). Again using construction adhesive, glue and nail the siding pieces to the swing support framework.

4. Install the conduit for the topmost rungs in the two short 4X4s (C) that you cut and drilled earlier. Bolt both C's in position against the upper arms (Q). The top of the C's should be level with the top of the B's; trim if necessary.

5. Cut the rafters (CC, DD) to length. Taper-cut the CC rafters, and nail them in place where shown in the Side Section and Construction Phase III drawings.

Bill of Materials

FOR PHASE III OF CONSTRUCTION

Part	Finished Size T	W	L	Mat.	Qty.
Z	⅝"	1'5"	2'1½"	4" grooved siding	1
AA	⅝"	2'	2'1½"	4" grooved siding	2
BB	⅝"	1'5"	2'0"	4" grooved siding	1
CC	1½"	3½"	1'9½"	2X4 (treated)	8
DD	1½"	3½"	1'2"	2X4 (treated)	4
EE	⅝"	5'0"	5'3½"	4" grooved siding	2
FF	⅝"	5'¼"	5'1½"	4" grooved siding	2
GG	¾"	1'9½"	5'1¼"	ext. plywood	2
HH	¾"	1'5"	1'10⅛"	ext. plywood	2
II	1½"	3½"	2'3"	2X4 (treated)	4
JJ	¾"	2'3"	2'3"	ext. plywood	1
KK	¾"	5½"	1'11"	white oak	1
LL	¾"	6" dia.		ext. plywood	2
MM	¾"	3" dia.		ext. plywood	2

Supplies: 7d galvanized box nails, 16d galvanized box nails, ¾" roofing nails, 8–60-lb. bags of concrete mix, 1–¾X18" threaded galvanized pipe with 2 pipe caps, 2–⅜X6" eyebolts/nuts/washers, 4–¼X1¼" eyebolts/nuts/washers, #10X1¼" flathead wood screws, 14–½X5½" carriage bolts/nuts/flat washers, ⅜X6" carriage bolts/nuts/flat washers, 50 sq. ft. of 90-lb. roll roofing, 4–10' lengths of galvanized roof edge, 2–3" plated strap hinges, ¾" dowel rod, 5–chain connectors, 25' of #2 straight link coil chain, 4–single block pulleys for ¼" rope, 50' of ¼" braided nylon for rigging and door handle, 1–plastic utility bucket, primer, paint, exterior construction adhesive, fibrated roofing cement, silicone caulk, exterior polyurethane

Applying the siding and roofing

1. Cut the siding (EE, FF) to size, making sure that each seam will center on a stud when butting the siding edge to edge. Cut the boom openings in each EE. Mark the 12" radius openings on the back side of each FF, and cut each to shape. The top of the siding should be flush with the top edge of the rafters. Glue and nail the siding in place. *Be sure to clinch over any exposed nails on the inside.*

2. Cut the plywood pieces (GG, HH) to fit the roof. The pieces should extend to the outer edges of the siding and cover the 2X4s of the upper roof opening. Glue and nail the plywood pieces in position.

3. Miter-cut the ends of the four roof members (II) and nail them in

continued

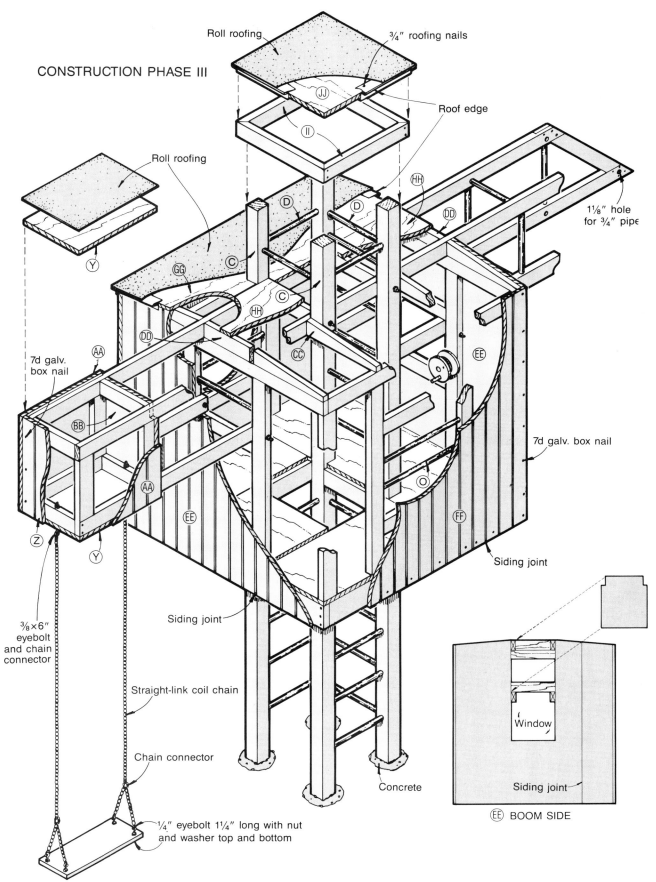

CONSTRUCTION PHASE III

Roll roofing

¾" roofing nails

Roof edge

Roll roofing

1⅛" hole for ¾" pipe

7d galv. box nail

7d galv. box nail

Siding joint

Siding joint

Concrete

⅜×6" eyebolt and chain connector

Straight-link coil chain

Chain connector

¼" eyebolt 1¼" long with nut and washer top and bottom

Window

Siding joint

(EE) BOOM SIDE

KIDS' PLAY STRUCTURE
continued

CRANE RIGGING

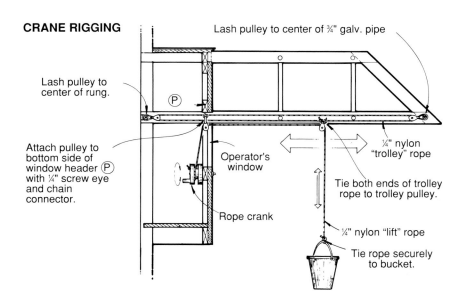

Lash pulley to center of ¾" galv. pipe

Lash pulley to center of rung.

Attach pulley to bottom side of window header Ⓟ with ¼" screw eye and chain connector.

Operator's window

Rope crank

¼" nylon "trolley" rope

Tie both ends of trolley rope to trolley pulley.

¼" nylon "lift" rope

Tie rope securely to bucket.

CRANK ASSEMBLY

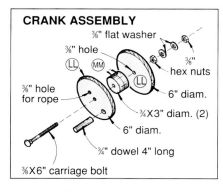

⅜" flat washer

⅜" hole

LL   MM

⅜" hole for rope

LL

⅜" hex nuts

6" diam.

¾×3" diam. (2)

6" diam.

¾" dowel 4" long

⅜×6" carriage bolt

place flush with the tops of B and C. Cut the plywood for the tower roof (JJ); then nail it in place.

4. Using tin snips, miter-cut the galvanized roof edge to length for the tower and main roof edges and nail them in place where shown.

5. Cut roll roofing for the tower, main roof, and the swing support. The roll roofing should sit flush with the edges of the galvanized roof edge. Apply a liberal coat of fibrated roofing cement to the roof edge and plywood; then nail it down. Caulk around the posts.

Attaching the swing
1. Using chain connectors, attach two lengths of chain to the eyebolts secured to the swing support. Cut

the lengths of chain to achieve the best height for your youngsters.

2. Cut the swing seat (KK) to size. Rout a ¼" round-over on the edges. Drill ¼" holes in the seat for four eyebolts. Fasten the eyebolts to the swing seat.

3. To ensure that the swing chair will sit level, start by cutting two 16" lengths of chain. Attach the chain to the pair of eyebolts at either end of the seat by spreading the eyes, slipping the chain into the eye, and reclosing the eyes.

4. Connect the chain connector to the middle link of both short lengths of chain connected to the swing chair. Attach the swing chair assembly to the two longer chains via the chain connectors.

Installing the cranelift rope
*Note: The crane is equipped with both a **lift rope** and a **trolley rope**. You raise the bucket by winding the lift rope on the rope crank. To move the trolley pulley from the outer end of the boom to the operator's window, you pull on the lower trolley rope. Position the trolley pulley before lifting the bucket. As a safety precaution, use the lift rope only with a bucket as*

shown in the Crane Rigging drawing at left. Do not replace the bucket with a hook or a loose rope end. This is to prevent children from accidentally getting tangled up or injured.

Also, we originally rigged the lift and trolley ropes as shown in the opening photo. After some time, and much play, we found that the ropes were getting tangled. We revised the rigging where shown in the Crane Rigging drawing for a more trouble-free system.

1. Cut the crank pieces (LL, MM) to size where shown in the Crank Assembly drawing *below left.* Construct the rope crank, gluing the parts together. Bolt the crank to the stud and siding so that it turns freely while firmly in place where shown in the Crane Rigging drawing.

2. Lash a pulley to the center of the pipe on the outer end of the boom where shown in the Crane Rigging drawing. Lash another pulley to the center of the rung that the lower boom notches around.

3. Rig up the lines and the pulleys where shown. As a safety measure, *do not* install any type of lock mechanism on the lift crank. This will ensure that the rigging always stays free-moving.

4. Prime and paint the siding and plywood as desired, being careful to paint all exposed edges to prevent damage from moisture. Apply several coats of exterior polyurethane to the swing seat.

Project Tool List
Radial-arm saw
    Dado blade or dado set
Portable circular saw
Portable jigsaw
Portable drill
Drill press
    Bits: ¼", ⅜", ½", ¾", ⅞", 1⅛"
Router
    ¼" round-over bit

Note: We built the project using the tools listed. You may be able to substitute other tools or equipment for listed items you don't have. Additional common hand tools and clamps may be required to complete the project.

WAGONS, HO!

Whether hauling building blocks or giving teddy bear a ride, this handsome four-wheeler will help your youngster get the job done. And you'll appreciate the wagon for its box-jointed corners, walnut trim, and sturdy hardwood construction.

Note: You'll need some thin stock for this project. You can either resaw or plane thicker stock to size. See the Buying Guide on page 15 for our wagon-hardware kit.

Start with the wagon-box sides

1. From ½"-thick maple, cut the box sides (A), and front and back (B) to the sizes listed in the Bill of Materials on *page 14.*

2. To box-joint the wagon-box pieces (A, B), start by fitting your tablesaw with a zero-clearance insert where shown in the Box-Joint Jig drawing on *page 12.* (Our Delta tablesaw requires a ½"-thick insert; we used plywood.)

3. Mount a ¼" dado blade to your tablesaw (we used a stackable blade). With the blade running, raise the rotating blade through the insert and ½" above the surface of the saw table. Elevate the blade
continued

CORNER DETAIL

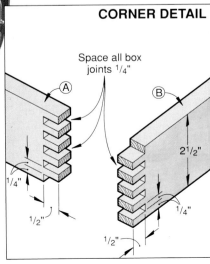

Space all box joints ¼"

Ⓐ   Ⓑ

2½"

¼"

½"   ¼"

½"

WAGONS, HO!
continued

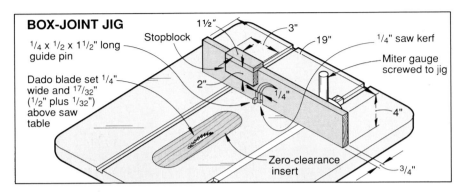

BOX-JOINT JIG

1/4 x 1/2 x 1 1/2" long guide pin

Stopblock

1 1/2"

3"

19"

1/4" saw kerf

Miter gauge screwed to jig

Dado blade set 1/4" wide and 17/32" (1/2" plus 1/32") above saw table

2"

1/4"

4"

Zero-clearance insert

3/4"

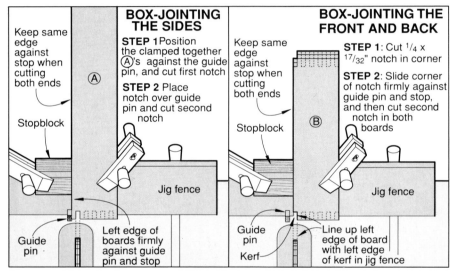

BOX-JOINTING THE SIDES

Keep same edge against stop when cutting both ends

STEP 1 Position the clamped together (A)'s against the guide pin, and cut first notch

STEP 2 Place notch over guide pin and cut second notch

(A)

Stopblock

Jig fence

Guide pin

Left edge of boards firmly against guide pin and stop

BOX-JOINTING THE FRONT AND BACK

Keep same edge against stop when cutting both ends

STEP 1: Cut 1/4 x 17/32" notch in corner

STEP 2: Slide corner of notch firmly against guide pin and stop, and then cut second notch in both boards

(B)

Stopblock

Jig fence

Guide pin

Kerf

Line up left edge of board with left edge of kerf in jig fence

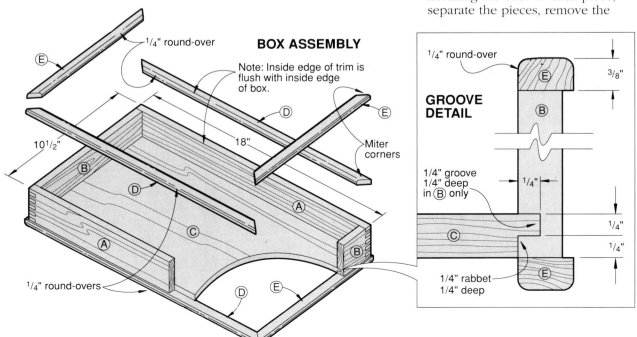

BOX ASSEMBLY

(E)

1/4" round-over

Note: Inside edge of trim is flush with inside edge of box.

(D)

(E)

10 1/2"

18"

Miter corners

(B)

(D)

(A)

(C)

(A)

(B)

1/4" round-overs

(D)

(E)

1/4" round-over

(E)

3/8"

GROOVE DETAIL

(B)

1/4"

1/4" groove 1/4" deep in (B) only

(C)

1/4"

1/4"

(E)

1/4" rabbet 1/4" deep

about 1/32" more (we found it is best to cut the fingers a bit long and sand them flush with the box sides after assembly).

4. Construct the jig and stopblock shown on the Box-Joint Jig drawing at *left*. The stopblock helps steady the long wagon sides, front, and back when cutting the box joints.

5. Carefully locate and cut a pair of 1/4"-wide kerfs 1/4" apart in the jig. For snug-fitting box joints, the kerfs and the distance between the guide pin and kerf must be exactly 1/4". Cut the guide pin to the size stated on the Box-Joint Jig drawing, and glue it into the kerf where shown on the drawing.

6. To box-joint the sides (A) simultaneously, tape the pieces together face-to-face with double-faced tape. Check that the edges and ends are flush. Repeat the taping procedure with the front and back pieces (B).

7. Follow the drawings at *left* to cut the notches in the side pieces, and then notch the front and back pieces. (To test the setup, we box-jointed scrap 1/2" stock before cutting the box pieces.) After notching the ends of each piece, separate the pieces, remove the

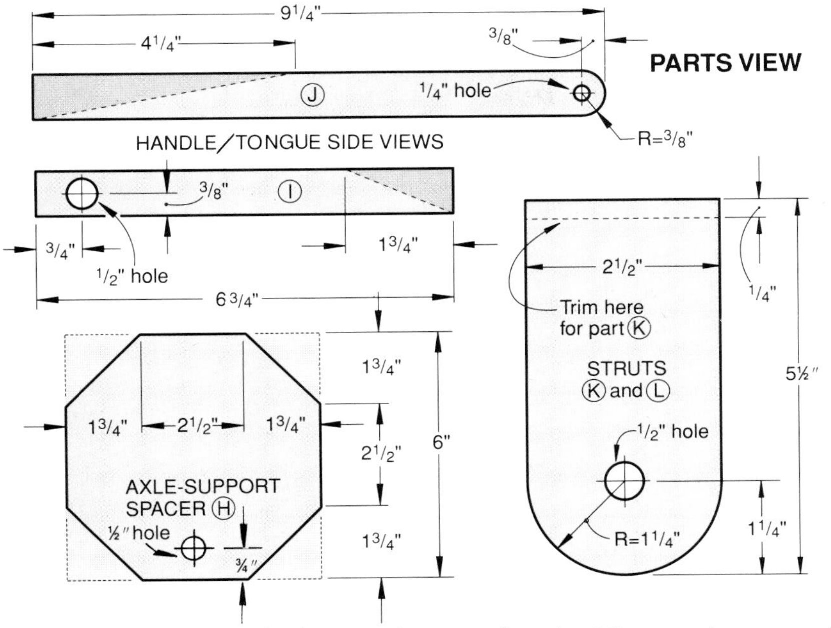
PARTS VIEW
9¹/₄"
4¹/₄"
³/₈"
J
¹/₄" hole
R=³/₈"
HANDLE/TONGUE SIDE VIEWS
³/₈"
I
³/₄"
¹/₂" hole
1³/₄"
6³/₄"
1³/₄"
1³/₄"
2¹/₂"
1³/₄"
2¹/₂"
6"
AXLE-SUPPORT
SPACER H
½" hole
¾"
1³/₄"
2¹/₂"
Trim here for part K
STRUTS K and L
¹/₄"
5½"
¹/₂" hole
R=1¹/₄"
1¹/₄"

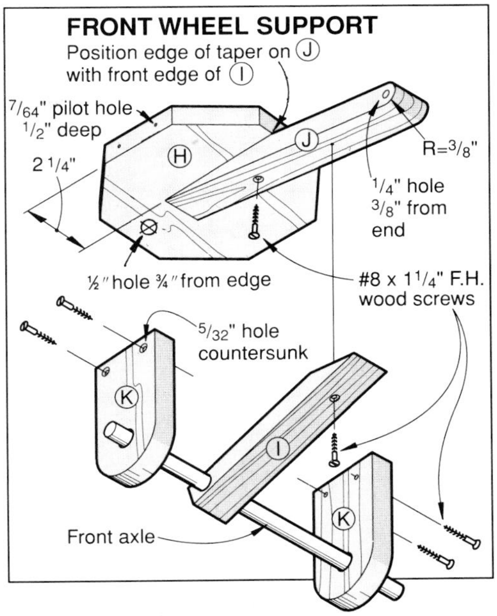
FRONT WHEEL SUPPORT
Position edge of taper on J with front edge of I
⁷/₆₄" pilot hole ¹/₂" deep
2¹/₄"
H
J
R=³/₈"
¹/₄" hole ³/₈" from end
½" hole ¾" from edge
#8 x 1¹/₄" F.H. wood screws
⁵/₃₂" hole countersunk
K
I
K
Front axle

tape, and sand smooth. (We used a thin, wedge-shaped piece of wood to pry apart the taped-together pieces. If necessary, use a splash of lacquer thinner to dissolve the adhesive, on the tape.)

Now, let's add the box bottom and trim pieces

1. Cut a ¼" groove ¼" deep along the inside bottom edge of the box front and back (B) where shown on the Box Assembly drawing and accompanying Groove detail *opposite, below*.

2. Edge-join ½" stock to form a 10×18" panel for the wagon bottom (C). Later, scrape off the excess glue, trim to size, sand smooth, and rout a ¼" rabbet ¼" deep along the ends (not the edges) of the wagon bottom.

3. Dry-fit the pieces (A, B, C) to check the fit.

4. Cover the mating surfaces of the box-joint fingers of pieces A and B with glue. (To allow the extended open time when applying the glue, we used white woodworker's glue and applied it with a ¼"-wide acid brush.) Glue and clamp the pieces (A, B, C), and check for square. Wipe off excess glue with a damp cloth.

5. Cut two pieces of ⅜" walnut to ⅝" wide by 5' long for trim pieces (D, E). Rout ¼" round-overs along the top edges of each strip. Miter-cut the top and bottom trim pieces (D, E) to length, and glue and clamp them to the box assembly with the inside edges flush where shown on the Box Assembly drawing and accompanying Groove detail.

Next, add the front and rear wheel supports

1. Cut the lazy-Susan spacer (F) to size from ⅜" plywood. Glue and clamp it to the box bottom.

2. Using the Parts View drawing *above* for reference, cut the steering stopblock (G) and axle-support spacer (H) to size. Cut the undercarriage tongue parts (I, J) to the sizes listed in the Bill of Materials.

3. Using the Parts View drawing for reference, mark the taper-cut lines on one edge of parts I and J. Bandsaw along the outside of each marked line, and then sand to the line to shape the pieces.

4. Referring to the Parts View drawing, mark the outlines and hole centerpoints for the axle struts (K, L), and cut them to size. Note that part K is ¼" shorter in length than part L. Next, drill the axle holes where marked.

5. Cut the rear-axle spacer (M) to size. Drill the mounting holes, and glue and screw the rear-axle struts (L) to the spacer (M).

6. Drill the mounting holes and assemble the front undercarriage assembly (H, I, J, K) in the manner shown on the Front-Wheel Support drawing *above*.

7. Drill pilot holes, and screw the lazy-Susan bearing to the support spacer (H). Rotate the bearing slightly, and fasten the other half of the bearing to the underside of the wagon box (F).

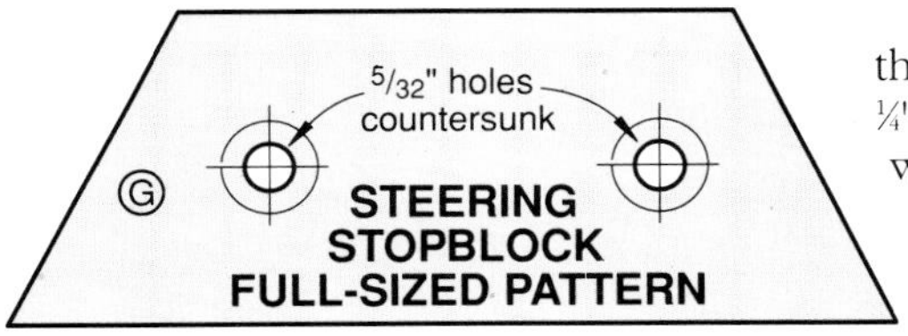
⁵/₃₂" holes countersunk
G
STEERING
STOPBLOCK
FULL-SIZED PATTERN

Add the handle for easy pulling

1. Cut the handle supports (N) to shape, using the five steps listed on the Handle-Support Blank drawing on *page 15*.

2. Cut the handle stem (O) to size. Drill a ½" hole ½" from one end where shown on the Exploded View drawing on *page 14*. Mark and cut a ½" radius on the same end as the hole for the handle dowel.

3. Glue the handle supports to the handle, being sure to keep the ¼" holes in the supports aligned with each other. Sand smooth.

4. Sand a slight round-over on all edges of the handle where

continued

WAGONS, HO!

continued

Note: You'll need to stick the end of your screwdriver through the ½" hole in the axle-support spacer (H) to gain access to the screw heads when screwing the lazy Susan bearing to the underside of the wagon box.

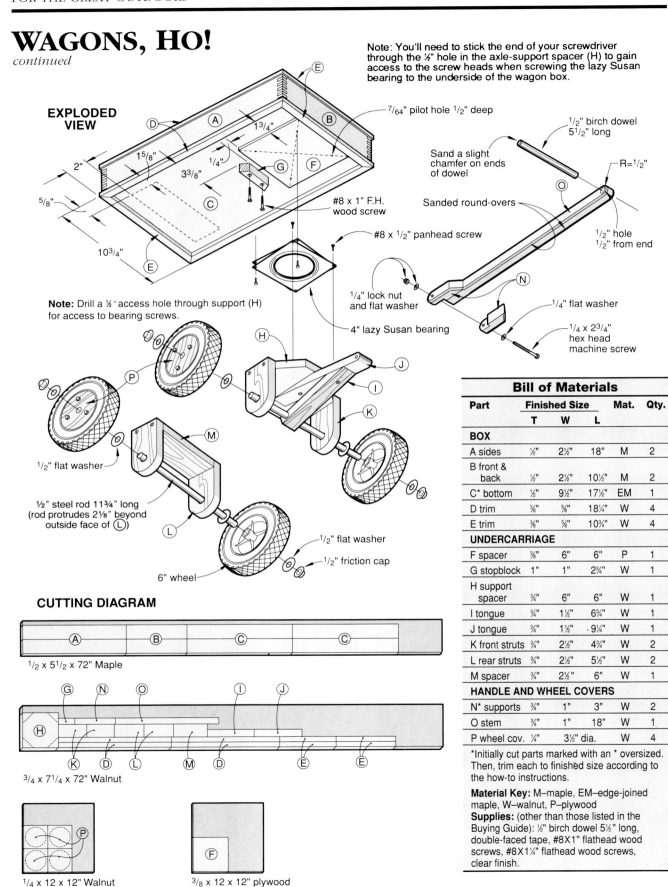

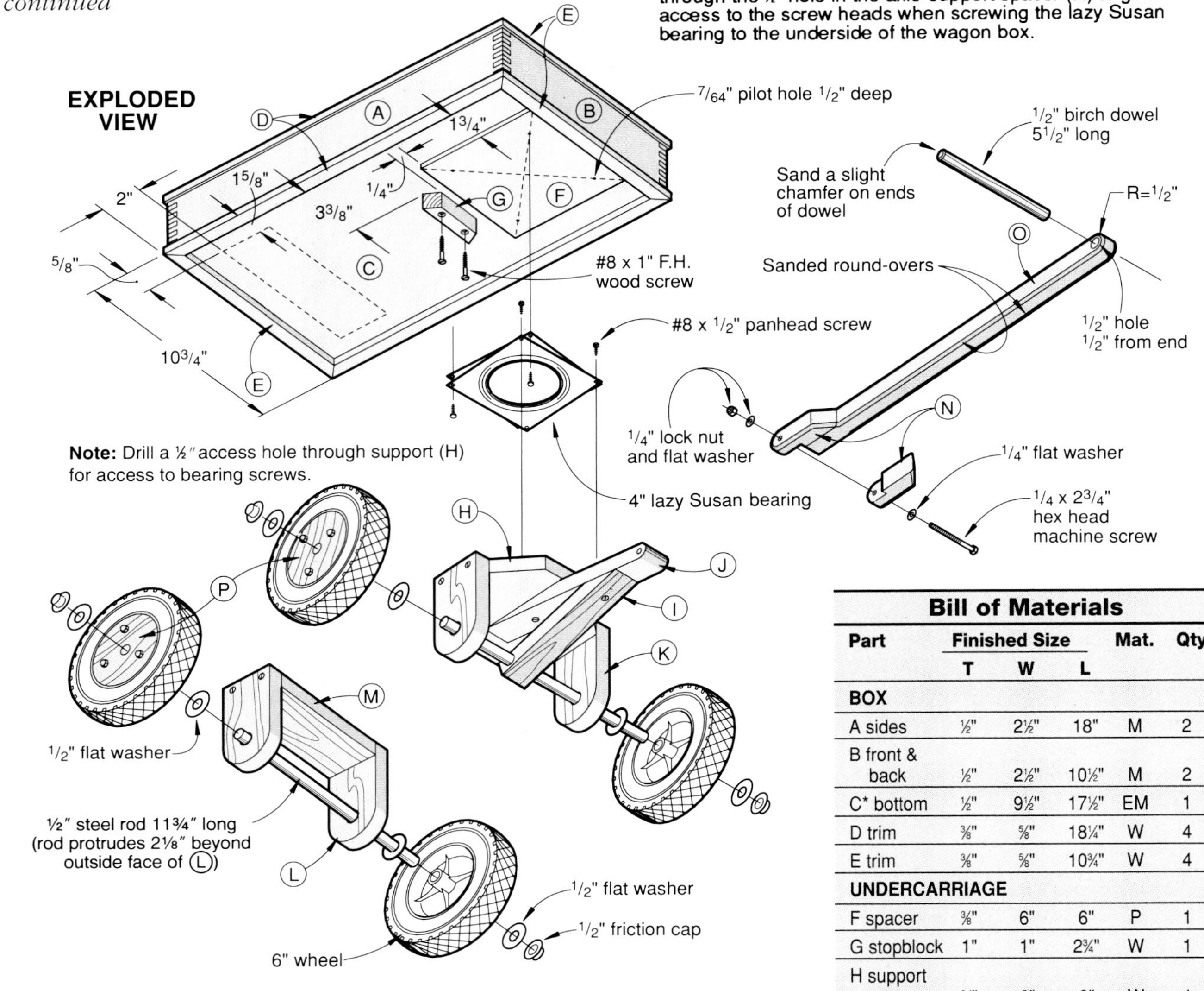
EXPLODED VIEW
A
B
C
D
E
F
G
1¾"
1⅝"
¼"
3⅜"
2"
⅝"
10¾"
7/64" pilot hole ½" deep
½" birch dowel 5½" long
Sand a slight chamfer on ends of dowel
R=½"
O
Sanded round-overs
½" hole ½" from end
#8 x 1" F.H. wood screw
#8 x ½" panhead screw
¼" lock nut and flat washer
N
¼" flat washer
¼ x 2¾" hex head machine screw
4" lazy Susan bearing
Note: Drill a ½" access hole through support (H) for access to bearing screws.
H
J
I
K
P
M
½" flat washer
½" steel rod 11¾" long (rod protrudes 2⅛" beyond outside face of L)
L
½" flat washer
½" friction cap
6" wheel

CUTTING DIAGRAM

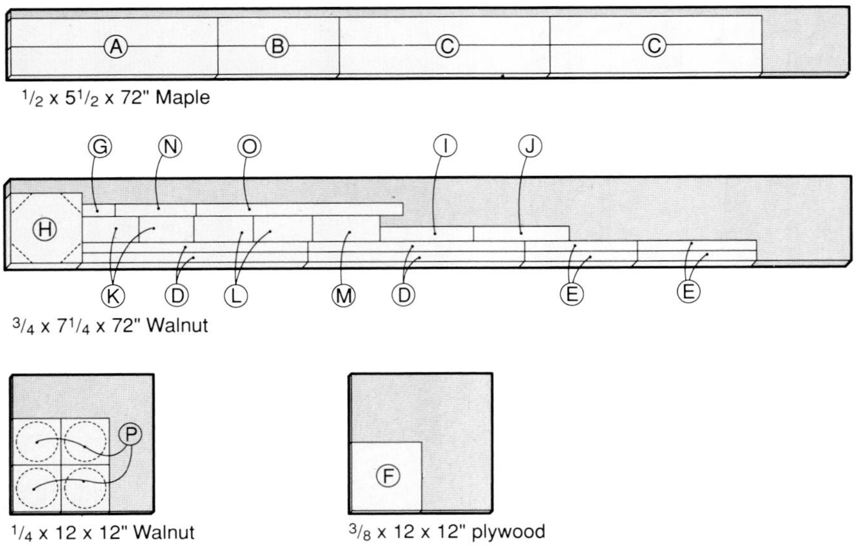
A
B
C
C
½ x 5½ x 72" Maple
G
N
O
I
J
H
K
D
L
M
D
E
E
¾ x 7¼ x 72" Walnut
P
¼ x 12 x 12" Walnut
F
⅜ x 12 x 12" plywood

Bill of Materials

Part	Finished Size T	W	L	Mat.	Qty.
BOX					
A sides	½"	2½"	18"	M	2
B front & back	½"	2½"	10½"	M	2
C* bottom	½"	9½"	17½"	EM	1
D trim	⅜"	⅝"	18¼"	W	4
E trim	⅜"	⅝"	10¾"	W	4
UNDERCARRIAGE					
F spacer	⅜"	6"	6"	P	1
G stopblock	1"	1"	2¾"	W	1
H support spacer	¾"	6"	6"	W	1
I tongue	¾"	1½"	6¾"	W	1
J tongue	¾"	1½"	9¼"	W	1
K front struts	¾"	2½"	4¾"	W	2
L rear struts	¾"	2½"	5½"	W	2
M spacer	¾"	2½"	6"	W	1
HANDLE AND WHEEL COVERS					
N* supports	¾"	1"	3"	W	2
O stem	¾"	1"	18"	W	1
P wheel cov.	¼"	3½" dia.		W	4

*Initially cut parts marked with an * oversized. Then, trim each to finished size according to the how-to instructions.

Material Key: M–maple, EM–edge-joined maple, W–walnut, P–plywood

Supplies: (other than those listed in the Buying Guide): ½" birch dowel 5½" long, double-faced tape, #8X1" flathead wood screws, #8X1¼" flathead wood screws, clear finish.

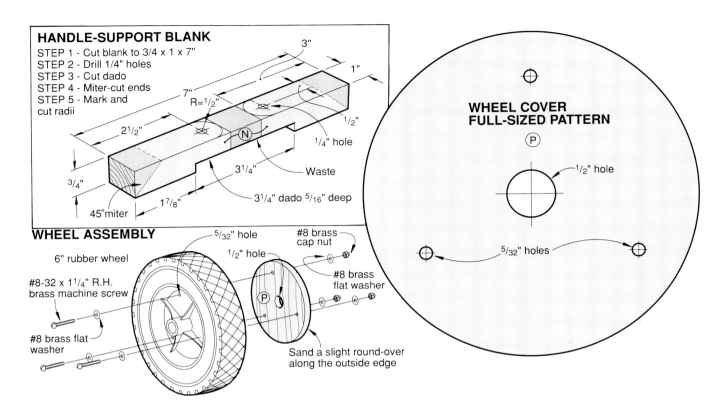

HANDLE-SUPPORT BLANK
STEP 1 - Cut blank to 3/4 x 1 x 7"
STEP 2 - Drill 1/4" holes
STEP 3 - Cut dado
STEP 4 - Miter-cut ends
STEP 5 - Mark and cut radii

3"
1"
7"
R=1/2"
1/2"
2 1/2"
N
1/4" hole
3 1/4" — Waste
3 1/4" dado 5/16" deep
3/4"
45° miter
1 7/8"

WHEEL COVER FULL-SIZED PATTERN
P
1/2" hole
5/32" holes

WHEEL ASSEMBLY
5/32" hole
#8 brass cap nut
6" rubber wheel
1/2" hole
#8-32 x 1 1/4" R.H. brass machine screw
#8 brass flat washer
P
#8 brass flat washer
Sand a slight round-over along the outside edge

shown on the Exploded View drawing.

5. Cut a ½" birch dowel to 5½" long. Sand a slight chamfer on the ends, and glue it in place in the ½" hole in the handle.

Now, for the wheel covers

1. Use a compass or the full-sized wheel-cover pattern to mark four 3½" circles on ¼" walnut plywood or solid stock for the wheel covers (P).

2. Cut the wheel covers to shape, cutting just outside the marked line. Now, sand to the line to finish the shaping. (We bandsawed the covers to shape, and then used our disc sander to sand to the line to finish the shaping.)

3. Transfer the ½" and ⁵⁄₃₂" hole centerpoints to each wheel cover, and then drill the holes where marked. (Using double-faced tape, we adhered the wheelcovers together face-to-face with the edges flush. Then, we used spray adhesive to adhere a photocopy of the wheel-cover pattern to the top piece. Next, we drilled through all four wheel covers at one time to

drill the ½" and ⁵⁄₃₂" holes. Finally, we pried apart the pieces with a wooden wedge, and removed the tape.)

It's almost playtime

1. Finish-sand, and apply the finish. For indoor use, we recommend polyurethane. For use outdoors, apply spar varnish.

2. Fasten the handle to tongue part (J). Fasten the wheel covers to the wheels where shown on the Wheel Assembly drawing *above*.

3. Using the Exploded View• drawing for reference, mount the wheels to the wagon.

Buying Guide

•**Wagon-hardware kit.** 4–6" diameter wheels; 2–½" steel rods 11¾" long with 4–½" friction caps and 8–½" flat washers; 4" lazy Susan with 8–#8x½" panhead wood screws; ¼x2¾" hex-head machine screw with 2–¼" flat washers and a ¼" lock nut; 12-8-32x1¼" round-head brass machine screws with 24–#8 brass flat washers and 12–#8 brass cap nuts. Kit no. WDWG. For current prices contact

Miller Hardware, 1300 Harding Road, Des Moines, IA 50314, or call 515-283-1724 to order.

Project Tool List
Tablesaw
  Dado blade or dado set
Bandsaw
Belt sander
Disc sander
Router
  ¼" round-over bit
Portable drill
Drill press
  Bits: ⁷⁄₆₄", ⁵⁄₃₂", ¼", ½"
Finishing sander

Note: *We built the project using the tools listed. You may be able to substitute other tools or equipment for listed items you don't have. Additional common hand tools and clamps may be required to complete the project.*

BUILD YOUR OWN BOOMERANG

The Seabreeze II Boomerang, a championship model designed by Chet Snouffer, guarantees you hours of fun for a minimal investment of time and material. Make several.

The beauty of boomerangs

Traveling at about 50 mph and revolving 10 times a second, the boomerang starts in a nearly vertical stance, like a speeding car tire. As it rotates, the lifting arm cuts through the air first and the trailing arm follows in the turbulence, with the result that each arm of the boomerang loses lift and airspeed. This phenomenon helps the boomerang keep its balance.

In the air, the boomerang exhibits fascinating behavior. At first vertical, it carves an arc through the sky to the thrower's left (or right, if thrown left-handed). Reaching the completed circumference of its path, the boomerang begins to lay down in a speeding horizontal position. Its circular journey completed, the boomerang hovers like a helicopter, ready to be caught.

On those summer afternoons when the sun starts its sultry decline, Chet's neighbors haul their lawn mowers out for a cool clip. But Chet hauls out his boomerangs and heads for the open fields.

"Once, my only concern was how little time the boomerang spent dilly-dallying along its path," notes Chet. "The less it hovered around, the faster it returned and the better it was for me in competition. What fascinates me now is the dipping, soaring, and hovering."

Whenever weather permits, Chet fits his boomeranging into the day. Competition still happens to be exciting to him, but other things

count even more—such as a boomerang brightened by the sun.

"A boomerang doesn't look like much sitting still, but when it's rotating, the thing has a unique beauty," Chet remarks, spinning his hand in the air. "Then, that piece of wood becomes a boomerang."

Note: *You'll need a 9x13x¼" (6 mm) piece of five- or seven-ply Baltic birch aircraft plywood (or good marine-grade plywood) to make your boomerang.*

1. Cutting out the blank

Using tracing paper, copy the full-sized boomerang pattern outlined here, including the bevel lines, and transfer it to the plywood. You can do this easily, and have clear lines to follow, if you place carbon paper under the pattern on the stock.

Situate your tracing-paper pattern on the stock so that the grain runs across the arms (as indicated by the wavy lines on the pattern); then trace the outline on the wood. Your wood will still work even if it has a warp to it, but you must trace the pattern and form the edges of the boomerang on the side of the stock that dishes upward.

Use a band saw, jigsaw, or scroll saw to cut out the boomerang blank from the plywood.

2. Marking the bevels

The top of the boomerang has two tapered edges, called *airfoils.* The leading edge has a 45° bevel, and the *trailing edge* has a 30° bevel (see pattern). Note that these edges blend into each other and gradually switch positions on the boomerang (i.e., the trailing edge of the right arm eventually becomes the leading edge on the left arm).

Where you position these edges on the boomerang determines if it will be left-handed or right-handed. Our pattern indicates edge positions for a right-handed boomerang. To make it left-handed, reverse the edge bevel positions: The trailing arm becomes the leading arm and its leading edge and trailing edge trade locations.

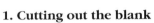

LEADING ARM

Cross-section view at this point

30° bevel on trailing edge

45° bevel on leading edge

This isn't as confusing as it first may seem, if you remember that a *leading edge* must cut the air first when you throw the boomerang. That's important, because otherwise it won't fly!

3. Shaping the boomerang

With a drum sander in a drill press, a disk sander in a portable drill, or by hand with a rasp, put a

45° bevel completely around the top side of the blank. Exactness isn't critical, so you can simply eyeball the bevel.

Next, sand back the bevel on the trailing edges as marked on the pattern until you have a 30° taper. Be sure to gradually blend trailing edges into leading edges. Refer to the boomerang-arm cross sections for the proper edge taper at both ends and in the center of the boomerang.

Finish sanding the edge contours by rounding off the 45° bevel of the leading edges to a bullnose. Turn the boomerang over and sand a slight tapering bevel along the leading edges for about 2½" from the tip of each arm, as indicated by the dashed line on the pattern. This bevel tends to add an even lift. Note the shape of the arm tips as indicated in the cross-section views.

4. Sanding and finishing

A smooth surface on your boomerang reduces wind resistance and makes catching much easier, so sand with 80-, then 120-grit paper.

Make your boomerang waterproof by applying sanding sealer. When dry, sand it again with 120-grit to smooth lifted grain fibers.

Let you imagination run when painting your boomerang. Bands of color or other decoration on the arms will create a pattern during the boomerang's flight. Whatever hue (or combination of hues) you choose, spray the color on for an even finish.

For added protection of the paint as well as the boomerang, spray it wth one or two coats of polyurethane or lacquer. Some throwers even rub a paste wax over the finished coat. But don't get carried away—too much finish adversely affects the boomerang's flight performance.

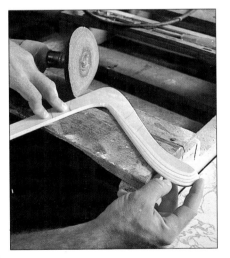

Chet Snouffer checks the smoothness of the tapering bevel on his boomerang's trailing edge. Note the plies exposed in the aircraft plywood blank.

TRAILING ARM

Cross-section view at this point

30° bevel on trailing edge

45° bevel on leading edge

Patterns broken for clarity, join when tracing.

SEABREEZE II BOOMERANG
(right-handed)
FULL SIZE PATTERN

Project Tool List

Bandsaw, scrollsaw, or jigsaw
Drum or disc sander

Note: We built the project using the tools listed. You may be able to substitute other tools or equipment for listed items you don't have. Additional common hand tools and clamps may be required to complete the project.

17

A KID'S RETREAT

Finally, a play structure that's good looking enough to occupy center stage in your backyard. Its size and diversity allow several kids to keep busy, yet it's simple enough to build in a couple of weekends. Two swings, plus a sandbox, plus a lookout tower add up to many summers of fun for creative youngsters.

Forming the framework

1. From 2x4 pressure-treated stock, cut the end support post parts (A, B) to the lengths listed in the Bill of Materials on *page 21.*

2. Mark centerlines—6" from center to center—for the decorative notches on one face of the shorter board (B) where shown on the Joint detail accompanying the Framework drawing. Now, mark a pair of notches at each centerline (we used the corner of a square to outline the notches). Cut the V-shaped notches with a jigsaw.

3. Sandwich the three boards together face to face, with the notched board in the middle where shown on the Joint detail. Drill ⅛" pilot holes and screw the three pieces together.

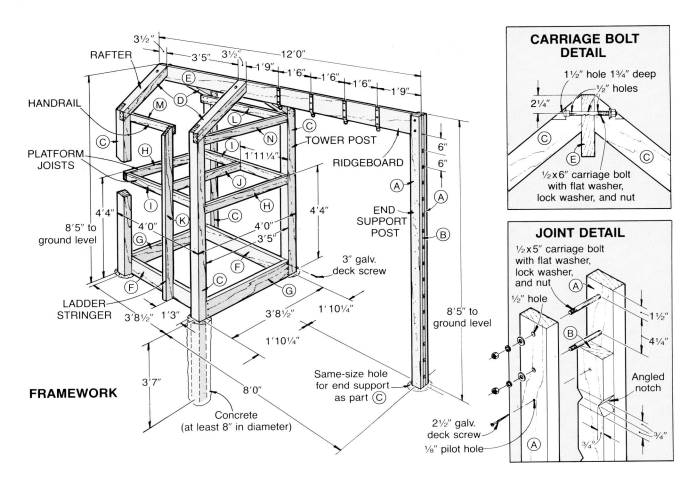

FRAMEWORK

RAFTER
HANDRAIL
PLATFORM JOISTS
8′5″ to ground level
LADDER STRINGER
3½″
3′5″
3½″
12′0″
1′9″
1′6″
1′6″
1′6″
1′9″
E
M
D
L
C
H
N
I
J
C
H
I
K
G
F
C
G
F
TOWER POST
RIDGEBOARD
END SUPPORT POST
4′4″
4′4″
4′0″
4′0″
1′11¼″
3′5″
6″
6″
A
A
B
3″ galv. deck screw
3′8½″
1′3″
3′8½″
1′10¼″
1′10¼″
3′7″
8′0″
8′5″ to ground level
Same-size hole for end support as part C
2½″ galv. deck screw
⅛″ pilot hole
A
Concrete (at least 8″ in diameter)

CARRIAGE BOLT DETAIL

1½″ hole 1¾″ deep
½″ holes
2¼″
C
E
C
½ x 6″ carriage bolt with flat washer, lock washer, and nut

JOINT DETAIL

½ x 5″ carriage bolt with flat washer, lock washer, and nut
½″ hole
A
B
1½″
4¼″
Angled notch
¾″
¾″

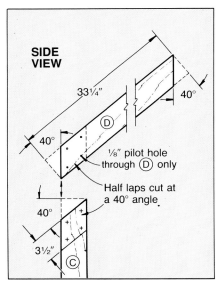

SIDE VIEW

33¼″
40°
40°
D
40°
40°
3½″
C
⅛″ pilot hole through D only
Half laps cut at a 40° angle.

4. From 4x4 treated stock, miter-cut the lookout-tower posts (C) and rafters (D) to the lengths listed in the Bill of Materials and shown on the Side View drawing *above*. Attach a dado blade to your radial

arm saw, and cut angled half laps where shown on the drawing. Screw the parts together to form each of the four frame components (C, D).

5. Cut the ridgeboard (E) to length. Using the dimensions on the Framework drawing *above* and Swing Support detail *below*, cut and bend four pieces of ¼″ steel strap around the ridgeboard where shown. Now, drill ¼″ holes through the steel strap and ridgeboard where shown in the swing support

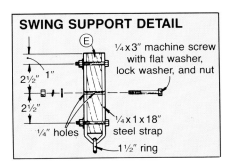

SWING SUPPORT DETAIL

E
¼ x 3″ machine screw with flat washer, lock washer, and nut
2½″
1″
2½″
¼″ holes
¼ x 1 x 18″ steel strap
1½″ ring

detail. Paint the steel strap, add a 1½″ ring to each support, and bolt each swing support in place.

6. Fit the ridgeboard into the notch in the top of the support post (A, B). Drill ½″ holes where shown on the Joint detail, and bolt the ridgeboard to the end support post, checking for square.

Dig the holes and assemble the framework

1. Using the dimensions on the Framework drawing, dig five holes 43″ deep. (We used a post-hole digger, and put the dirt on tarps for easy cleanup later.)

2. Temporarily nail the posts together where shown on *page 20, top left*. Repeat for the second frame.

3. With a helper, stand one of the frames upright in the holes. Repeat for the second frame.

4. Again with a helper, stand the ridgeboard and end support
continued

A KID'S RETREAT
continued

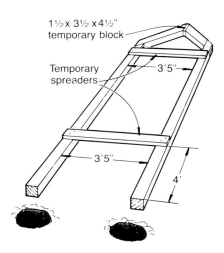

1½ x 3½ x 4½"
temporary block

Temporary
spreaders

3'5"

3'5"

4'

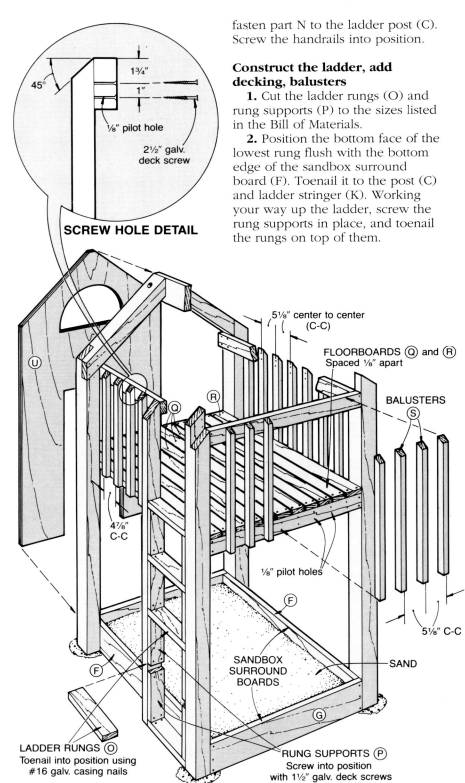

45°

1¾"

1"

⅛" pilot hole

2½" galv.
deck screw

SCREW HOLE DETAIL

5⅛" center to center
(C-C)

FLOORBOARDS Ⓠ and Ⓡ
Spaced ⅛" apart

Ⓤ

Ⓡ

Ⓠ

BALUSTERS
Ⓢ

4⅞"
C-C

⅛" pilot holes

Ⓕ

5⅛" C-C

Ⓕ

SANDBOX
SURROUND
BOARDS

SAND

Ⓕ

Ⓖ

LADDER RUNGS Ⓞ
Toenail into position using
#16 galv. casing nails

RUNG SUPPORTS Ⓟ
Screw into position
with 1½" galv. deck screws

assembly (A, B, E) in the last hole. Knock the 2×4 scrap spacers from between the rafters (D), and fit the ridgeboard into place (you'll need a stepladder for this). Nail the ridgeboard in position flush with the top edges of the rafters.

5. Being careful to miss the nails, drill and counterbore holes through each rafter and through the ridgeboard using the hole sizes shown on the Carriage Bolt Detail on *page 19.* (We used an electrician's bit to drill the long ½"-diameter hole, and counterbored with a Forstner bit.) Bolt the roof parts together.

6. Check that the tower posts are plumb in both directions and the ridgeboard is level. Mix and pour concrete into the holes.

Adding the horizontal framing

1. Cut the sandbox surround boards (F, G) to size, and screw them to the posts where shown on the Framework drawing.

2. Cut the platform joists (H, I) to size, and screw them to the tower posts, checking for level. Measure the distance, and cut the middle joist (J) to length. Screw the middle joist into position.

3. Miter-cut the ladder stringer (K) to length. Screw it to the sandbox surround (F) and platform joist (I), checking for plumb.

4. Finally, cut the handrails (L, M, N) to length. Cut a 2×2 cleat to

fasten part N to the ladder post (C). Screw the handrails into position.

Construct the ladder, add decking, balusters

1. Cut the ladder rungs (O) and rung supports (P) to the sizes listed in the Bill of Materials.

2. Position the bottom face of the lowest rung flush with the bottom edge of the sandbox surround board (F). Toenail it to the post (C) and ladder stringer (K). Working your way up the ladder, screw the rung supports in place, and toenail the rungs on top of them.

3. Cut the platform decking (Q, R) to size. (We ripped part R to width from a 2×6.) Drill ⅛" pilot holes and screw the pieces in place, spacing them ⅛" apart. (We cut spacers ⅛" thick to position the decking pieces correctly before fastening them to the joists.)

4. Miter-cut 18 balusters (S) to length from 2×2 stock. Using the center-to-center (c-c) dimensions on the Final Assembly drawing, position the balusters, drill the pilot holes, and screw the balusters to the joists and handrails.

Adding the threshold and facade

1. Cut the threshold (T) to size. Mark and cut a notch in each end where shown on the Threshold drawing at *right*. Screw the threshold to the sandbox surround.

2. Using the Facade End View *below right* for reference, mark the window and door openings on a 4×8 sheet of exterior plywood for the facade (U). Cut the openings to shape with a jigsaw.

3. Position the facade on the threshold and against the end framework, and temporarily nail it into position against the framework. Now, get up on the platform, trace the roof outline onto the back side of the plywood facade. Remove the facade from the framework, support it on sawhorses, and cut the marked roof outline to shape.

4. Prime and paint the bottom edge of the facade. After the paint dries, nail the facade to the framework.

5. Using a belt sander, sand the edges of the facade flush with the outside edges of the 4×4 framework. Sand the plywood edges at the door and window openings.

6. Prime and paint the facade as desired, being careful to paint all exposed plywood edges several times to prevent moisture damage later. Now, paint the door and window outlines as dimensioned on the Facade drawing.

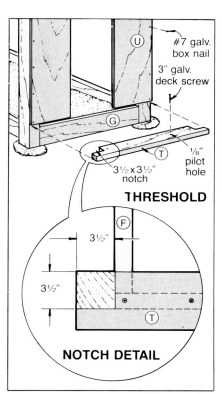

THRESHOLD

NOTCH DETAIL

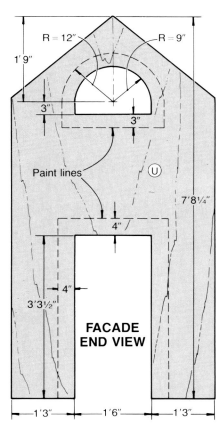

FACADE END VIEW

Part	Finshed Size			Mat.	Qty.
	T	W	L		
BASIC FRAMEWORK					
A	1½"	3½"	12'	2×4 (treated)	2
B	1½"	3½"	11' 4¾"	2×4 (treated)	1
C	3½"	3½"	10' 7½"	4×4 (treated)	4
D	3½"	3½"	2' 9¼"	4×4 (treated)	4
E	1½"	7¼"	12'	2×8 (treated)	1
TOWER FRAMING					
F	1½"	7¼"	3' 9"	2×8 (treated)	2
G	1½"	7¼"	3' 5"	2×8 (treated)	2
H	1½"	3½"	3' 5"	2×4 (treated)	2
I	1½"	3½"	3' 9"	2×4 (treated)	2
J	1½"	3½"	3' 2"	2×4 (treated)	1
K	1½"	3½"	6' 8"	2×4 (treated)	1
L	1½"	3½"	3' 10½"	2×4 (treated)	1
M	1½"	3½"	2' 5½"	2×4 (treated)	1
N	1½"	3½"	3' 5"	2×4 (treated)	1
FINAL ASSEMBLY					
O	1½"	3½"	1' 3"	2×4 (treated)	5
P	¾"	3½"	11⅞"	1×4 (treated)	8
Q	1½"	3½"	4'	2×4 (treated)	10
R	1½"	4¾"	4'	2×6 (treated)	1
S	1½"	1½"	2' 7¼"	2×2 (treated)	18
T	1½"	5½"	4'	2×6 (treated)	1
U	¾"	4'	7' 8¼"	ext. plywood	1
V	1½"	5½"	1' 7½"	2×6 (treated)	2

Supplies: 1½", 2½", and 3 " galvanized deck screws, #7 galvanized box nails, #16 galvanized casing nails, 2–½ X6" carriage bolts with nuts and washers, 2–½ X5" carriage bolts with nuts and washers, 12–¼ X3" machine screws with nuts and washers, 4 pieces of ¼X1X18" steel strap, 4–1½" rings, 8–¼X2 ½" eyebolts with 16–¼" nuts and washers, 34' of #2 straight-link coil chain, 16–chain-link connectors, 12–60-lb. bags of concrete, exterior primer, and paint, 49 ¾ X63" material for roof (dimensions are before hemming), 6–¼" grommets, 6-mm plastic, sand.

Now for the swings

1. Cut the two swing seats (V) to size from 2×6 stock. Rout a ⅜" round-over on all edges, and then sand the seats smooth.

2. Using the dimensions and hole sizes on the Swing drawing on *page 22*, drill the holes, and attach the ¼X2½" eyebolts to each seat.

3. Using chain connectors, attach four lengths of chain to the rings strapped to the ridgeboard. Cut the lengths of chain to achieve the best seat height for your youngsters.

continued

A KID'S RETREAT
continued

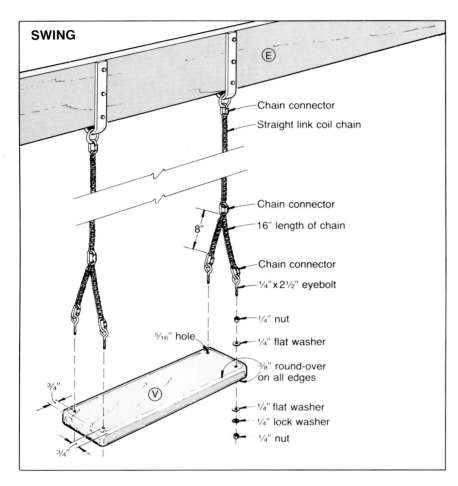

SWING

Chain connector
Straight link coil chain
Chain connector
16" length of chain
8"
Chain connector
¼" x 2½" eyebolt
¼" nut
5⁄16" hole
¼" flat washer
3⁄8" round-over on all edges
¾"
¼" flat washer
¼" lock washer
¼" nut
¾"

Ⓔ
Ⓥ

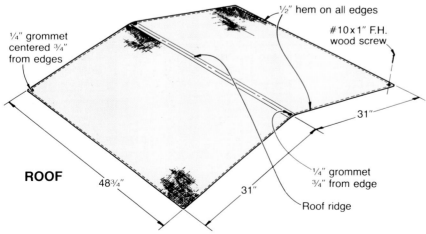

ROOF

½" hem on all edges
#10 x 1" F.H. wood screw
¼" grommet centered ¾" from edges
31"
¼" grommet ¾" from edge
48¾"
31"
Roof ridge

4. To ensure that the swing seats will sit level, start by cutting two 16" lengths of chain, making sure you have an odd number of links. With chain connectors, attach the chain to the pair of eyebolts at each end of the swing seat.

5. Connect a chain connector to the middle link of each 16" length of chain. Attach the 16" lengths to the ends of the long lengths with chain connectors where shown on the Swing drawing.

Fill the sandbox and call the kids

1. Belt-sand all sharp edges, especially those around the ladder.

2. Cover the floor and interior surfaces of the sandbox surround boards with 6-mm plastic. Cut small slits in the plastic to let any water drain out. Fill the box with sand.

Options: *Add house numbers, a gravel sidewalk, a roof, and plants, if desired. If you plan to add the roof, see the drawing above for details. (We used Sunbrella—a fade-resistant awning material; canvas also would work. Check the hemming and grommeting prices at a nearby awning shop.)*

Project Tool List
Radial-arm saw
    Dado blade or dado set
Portable circular saw
Portable jigsaw
Portable drill
    Bits: ⅛", ¼", ½", 1½"
    Electrician's bit, ½"
Belt sander
Router
    ⅜" round-over bit

Note: *We built the project using the tools listed. You may be able to substitute other tools or equipment for listed items you don't have. Additional common hand tools and clamps may be required to complete the project.*

BIG-LEAGUE ORGANIZER

When your favorite ball player slides in the door, gear should pop up on this handy-dandy rack. And when the little slugger connects at home, all of his fans will cheer.

Let's prepare the diamond first

1. Cut a 16×16" piece of ½" plywood. (We used birch.) With the grain running vertically, draw a line ½" above and parallel to the bottom edge. Mark its centerpoint. From it, scribe a vertical centerline the length of the piece.

2. Using the dimensions on the Plaque drawing on *page 24,* lay out the sides radiating 45° from the base centerpoint, and the pivot point 6⅞" up from the base.

3. On a piece of ¼"×¾"×12" scrap wood, mark a centerpoint ½" from the end, and a second one, 7½" from that point. Next, drive ¾"×17 brads ⅛" through both points, and lightly tap the second one into the pivot point on the plywood. Now, use it as a compass as shown *below,* and scribe the arc for the top of the diamond.

4. Plot the centerpoints for the Shaker peg holes. Drill the holes. (We purchased the pegs at a local homecenter store.) Back the board with scrap to prevent chip-out.

5. Bandsaw the board to shape. (We cut just outside the line, and then sanded to the line.)

6. Cut a strip of ¾"-wide birch plywood edging long enough to surround the board. (We purchased the edging at a local homecenter store.) Apply contact cement to the edge of the plywood piece, and to the edging strip. Adhere the edging to the board. Trim the excess edging with a razor blade. Lightly sand the edges and joint.

Next, make the shelf

1. Rip and crosscut the 3½×8½" shelf from ¾" birch stock. Using the dimensions on the Shelf drawing on *page 24,* lay out the centerpoints for the holes, the 1⅛"-wide slot, and all rounded corners.

2. Bore the 1⅝" and 2" holes. (We used Forstner bits. If you don't have bits this size, use a circle cutter or scrollsaw.) Saw the bat's slot. Saw and then sand the ⅜" and ¾" corner radii.

3. Rout a round-over along the top edge of the front, the ends, and the two holes and slot. Do not round over the back edge. Finish-sand the piece.

4. On the plaque's back, lay out the centerpoints for the two keyhole slots where dimensioned on the Plaque drawing. Rout the slots with a keyhole slot-cutting bit to ⁵⁄₁₆" depth. Mark the centerpoints for the shelf screws. Drill ⁵⁄₃₂" pilot holes and countersink them.

Now, paint and finish your plaque

1. Make two full-sized copies of the Diamond half-pattern on *page 25.* To do this, fold a sheet of tracing paper in half and place the fold along the pattern's centerline. Tape it in place, and trace the half pattern onto the paper. Next, remove the tracing paper, turn it over, and duplicate the tracing on that side of the paper. Now, unfold the paper.

2. Cut one copy for a paint mask, removing everything except the baselines, the home plate circle, and the three pie-shaped bases. Spray adhesive to the back and place it on the plywood, using dimensions on the Plaque drawing for placement.

3. Spray-paint the plaque green. (We applied three light coats.) Now, remove the paper mask.

4. To prepare the base paths for painting, cut out the area inside the baselines and the area around home plate on the *second* pattern. Cut out home plate. Adhere it to the face of the board, aligning the points with the horizontal reference line and the vertical centerline. To form the base paths, place strips of masking tape ³⁄₁₆" away and parallel to the paper mask.

5. Drive a brad through your shop-made compass 6⅞₁₆" from the end. Position the brad on the pivot point. Now, while holding a pencil at the end of the compass, lightly strike an arc for aligning the bottoms of the letters.

6. With carbon paper, transfer the "Little Slugger" letters found on *page 25* onto thin cardboard (we used a manila folder), and cut out the letter openings with a razor blade. Arrange the letters on the reference line drawn in Step 5, and outline them lightly with pencil.

7. Paint the letters, bases, and base path white. (We used acrylic artist's paint and carefully brushed it on between the masks with a #6 flat artist's brush.) After the paint dries, remove the masking pattern and tape. Erase any pencil lines from the unpainted areas. Finish the birch shelf and the two Shaker pegs. (We applied two coats of clear lacquer.) Apply two coats of clear finish to the painted field.

8. Screw the shelf to the front of the board. (We used #6×1¼" flathead wood screws.) Glue the Shaker pegs in the holes. Drive two #8×2" flathead wood screws into the wall 10¾" apart, and at the same height. Let the screw heads extend ¼" from the wall. Now, hang the plaque on the screws.

continued

23

BIG-LEAGUE ORGANIZER
continued

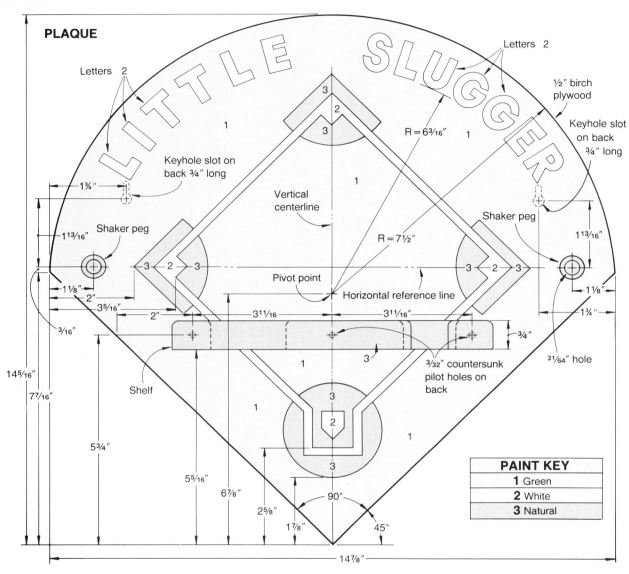

PLAQUE

Letters 2

Letters 2

Keyhole slot on back ¾" long

R = 6³⁄₁₆"

½" birch plywood

Keyhole slot on back ¾" long

1¾"

Vertical centerline

Shaker peg

1¹³⁄₁₆"

Shaker peg

R = 7½"

1¹³⁄₁₆"

1⅛"

Pivot point

Horizontal reference line

1⅛"

3⁵⁄₁₆"

2"

3¹¹⁄₁₆"

3¹¹⁄₁₆"

1¾"

³⁄₁₆"

¾"

31⁄64" hole

14⁵⁄₁₆"

³⁄₃₂" countersunk pilot holes on back

7⁷⁄₁₆"

Shelf

5¾"

5⁵⁄₁₆"

6⁷⁄₈"

2⅝"

90°

1⅞"

45°

14⅞"

PAINT KEY	
1	Green
2	White
3	Natural

Project Tool List
Tablesaw
Bandsaw
Disc sander
Drill press
   Bits: ³⁄₃₂", ³⁄₆₄", 1⅛", 2"
Router
   Bits: ¼" round-over, keyhole slot-cutter
Finishing sander

Note: *We built the project using the tools listed. You may be able to substitute other tools or equipment for listed items you don't have. Additional common hand tools and clamps may be required to complete the project.*

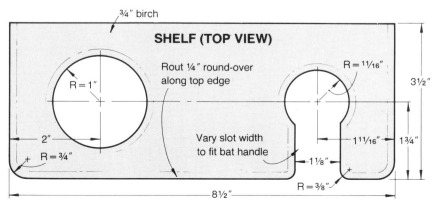

¾" birch

SHELF (TOP VIEW)

Rout ¼" round-over along top edge

R = 1"

R = 1¹⁄₁₆"

3½"

2"

1¹¹⁄₁₆"

1¾"

R = ¾"

Vary slot width to fit bat handle

1⅛"

R = ⅜"

8½"

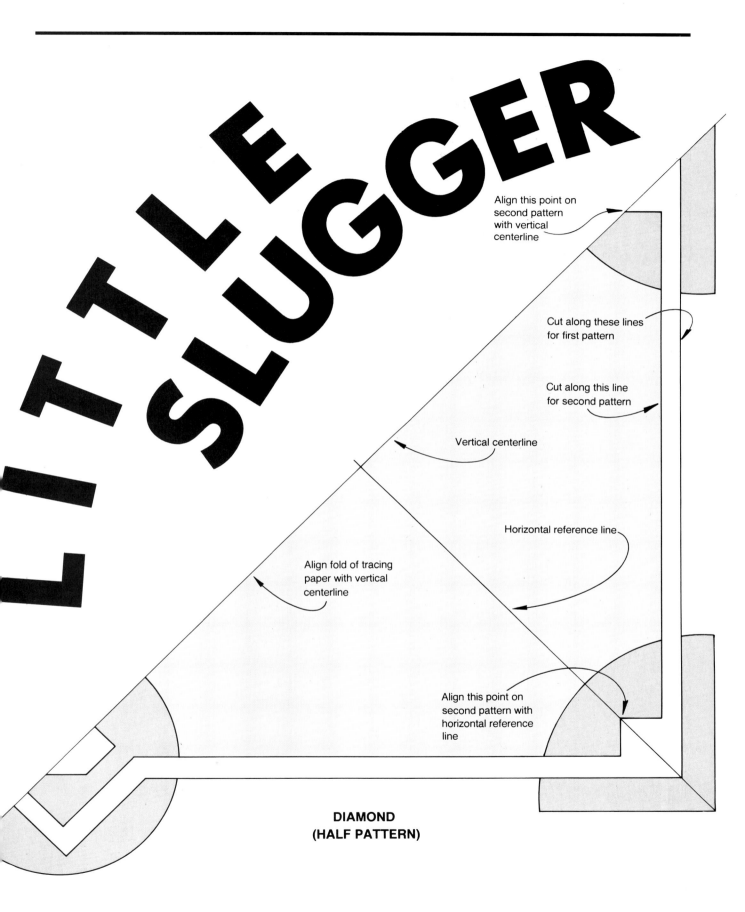

LITTLE SLUGGER

Align this point on second pattern with vertical centerline

Cut along these lines for first pattern

Cut along this line for second pattern

Vertical centerline

Horizontal reference line

Align fold of tracing paper with vertical centerline

Align this point on second pattern with horizontal reference line

DIAMOND
(HALF PATTERN)

BIG-HIT BASEBALL BAT

When we decided to feature a baseball bat we went straight to the experts, Hillerich and Bradsby Co., the makers of the renowned Louisville Slugger®. The folks at H&B turn wood bats for a living (among other things), making over a million of them a year from ash. Why ash? It's because this wood offers the proper amount of tensile strength, weight, and resiliency desired in a finished bat. In short, ash puts 'em on base and drives 'em home. If you can't buy ash locally, use our Buying Guide to mail order a turning square or two.

Turn the square round

1. Start with a 3×3" ash turning square at least 31" long. (See the Buying Guide for our source.)

2. Mark diagonals on each end of the square to locate centers. Next, mount the square between centers on your lathe.

3. Using a gouge or a skew, and a speed of about 800–1,000 rpm, round down the turning stock to a 2¾"-diameter cylinder. See the drawing *below* for tool position if you round down the stock with a gouge. After rounding the stock, stop the lathe and move the tool rest closer to the cylinder. (For long smooth cuts and less readjusting, we used

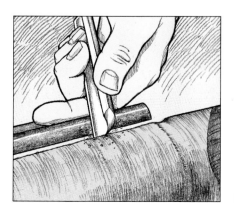

the longest [12"] tool rest that we had available.)

Next, turn the bat to rough shape

1. Refer to the dimensions on Step 1 of the Two-Step drawing *opposite,* and mark the depth-reference points on the cylinder where shown.

2. Using a parting tool and an outside caliper, make all of the depth-reference cuts into the cylinder on the marks you just scribed. While making these cuts, stop the lathe frequently and check the diameter of the cylinder within each cut with the caliper. *Do not* cut too deeply. Allow extra stock for the finish cuts, and sanding.

3. Remove the wood between the reference cuts. Again, do not cut deeper than the reference cuts at this time. (As shown *below,* we used a 1" skew chisel for this. A spindle gouge would also work.)

4. Using the skew or a spindle gouge, form the knob on the handle end. Next, move the tool rest to the opposite end, and carefully round-over the fat end of the bat. Leave the tenons on each end of the bat (ours measured about

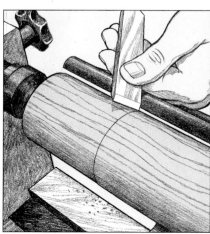

TWO–STEP DRAWING

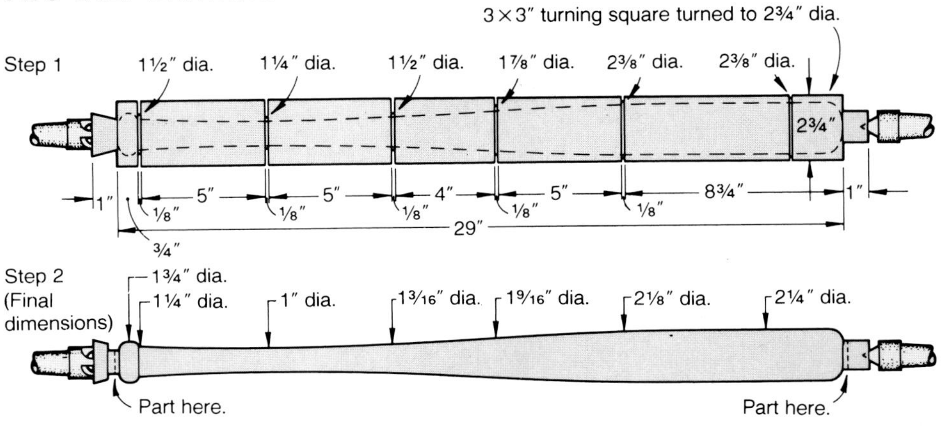

3 × 3" turning square turned to 2¾" dia.
Step 1
1½" dia.
1¼" dia.
1½" dia.
1⅞" dia.
2⅜" dia.
2⅜" dia.
2¾"
1"
5"
5"
4"
5"
8¾"
1"
⅛"
⅛"
⅛"
⅛"
⅛"
29"
¾"
Step 2 (Final dimensions)
1¾" dia.
1¼" dia.
1" dia.
1 3/16" dia.
1 9/16" dia.
2⅛" dia.
2¼" dia.
Part here.
Part here.

TWO-STEP LETTERING

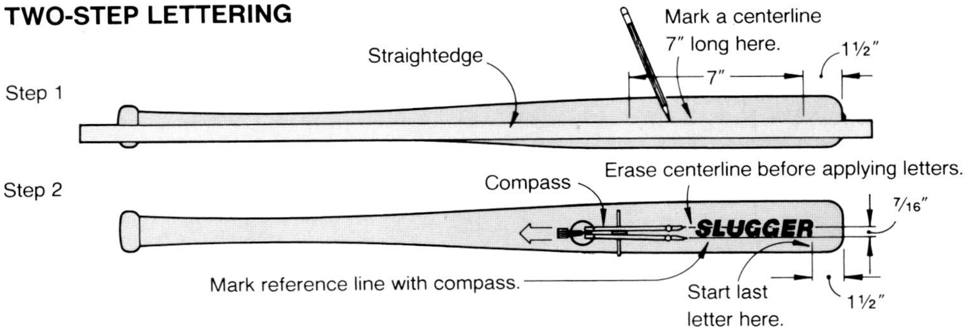

Mark a centerline 7" long here.
Straightedge
1½"
7"
Step 1
Step 2
Erase centerline before applying letters.
Compass
7/16"
SLUGGER
Mark reference line with compass.
Start last letter here.
1½"

1¼" in diameter). You'll remove them later.

Make the final cuts, and sand the bat

1. Increase lathe speed to 1,200 –1,500 rpm, and make long, smooth finish cuts with the skew. Stop frequently to check the bat diameters with an outside caliper against the final dimensions shown on the Step 2 drawing, *above*.

2. Machine-sand the bat. (We chucked a 2" flexible rubber disc into our portable drill to sand the bat as shown *below*. Hold your drill so the disc rotates *into* the turning

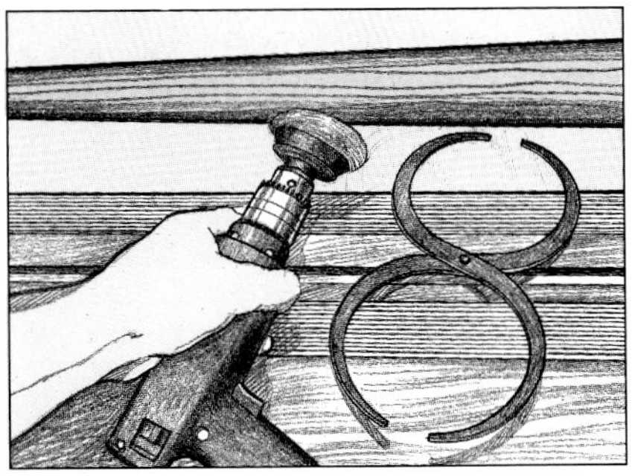

as the latter spins.) Or, hand-sand the bat.

3. Make the parting cuts at each end of the bat. (We worked back and forth until each tenon measured less than ¼" diameter. Next, we sanded as much of the ends as we could, then stopped the lathe and finished cutting the tenons with a fine-toothed saw.) Finally, finish-sand the tenons flush with the ends.

4. To apply the SLUGGER® name (see the Buying Guide for our source, or buy a sheet of similar dry-transfer letters at an art supply store), lightly mark a 7"-long reference centerline on the face grain at the fat end of the bat. Step 1 on the Two-Step Lettering drawing *above* shows how we did this. Next, mark a line 7/16" below the centerline where shown on the Step 2 drawing. Now, scribe a perpendicular start line 1½" from the end of the bat. Erase the centerline.

5. Place the sheet with the name SLUGGER® over the bat and align the bottoms of the letters along the reference line, and the letter R with the start line. Tape the sheet in place with masking tape. Next, carefully rub the face of the letter R with the burnishing tool provided to transfer it onto the bat. Transfer the remaining letters onto the bat using the same technique. Erase the lines.

6. Apply the finish. (We sprayed on three coats of exterior polyurethane. Apply light coats so you do not disturb the lettering.) Sand the finish lightly between coats.

Buying Guide

- **Ash turning square.** 3x3x36" ash turning square. Order no. WA3336. For current price, contact Constantines, 2050 Eastchester Road, Bronx, NY 10461.
- **Letters and tool.** Two SLUGGER® emblems (dry-transfer letters of 84-point, Helvetica Bold Italic), burnishing tool, and application instructions. For current prices, contact The Art Store, 600 Harding Rd., Des Moines, IA 50312.

SLUGGER® is a registered trademark of the Hillerich and Bradsby Company, Louisville, KY.

Supplies

Polyurethane finish.

Project Tool List

Lathe
- Spindle gouge
- Skew
- Parting tool

Portable drill
- Sanding disc

Note: *We built the project using the tools listed. You may be able to substitute other tools or equipment for listed items you don't have. Additional common hand tools and clamps may be required to complete the project.*

PINT-SIZED PICNIC TABLE

If you get a kick out of seeing kids' faces light up with delight, wait until you give that special someone this special something. Just the right size for a cookout with Mom and Dad, or for a little summertime tea-partying or bubble-blowing, this durable creation requires only four 16-foot 2×4s and a few dollars' worth of hardware to build.

Note: We used pressure-treated lumber for this project, but you could use redwood, cedar, or cypress with equal success. The wood you choose depends on the final look you prefer and your
budget for this project. Cut the pieces as indicated in the Cutting Diagram below *to get all the parts from four 2×4s.*

Assembling the tabletop

1. Using 2×4 stock, cut the tabletop pieces (A) and tabletop supports (B, C) to length. Trim the
bottom ends of the tabletop supports at a 45° angle as shown in the Exploded View drawing *opposite.* Cut the angled aluminum stock to size and file off any sharp edges.

2. Rip a strip of scrap stock to ⅝" then cut it into 2" lengths for later use as spacers.

3. Set the ¾" pieces of aluminum that you cut in step 1 on each side of each tabletop support (B). Drill pilot holes and screw the aluminum to the supports using #8×1¼" wood screws.

4. Choose the best face of the top pieces (A) and lay them facedown on the floor. Insert the scrap spacers between the tabletop pieces, and clamp the assembly together (make sure the ends of A are flush). Position the tabletop supports 7" in from each end of the tabletop, then using #8×1¼" wood screws, fasten the two supports to the tabletop.

5. Mark the center between the supports, then position and screw the center support (C) to the underside of the table at that point using #10×2" wood screws.

Attaching the legs

1. Cut the seat supports (D) and seats (E) to length; cut the legs (F) to length plus 2". Then, fashion the diagonal braces (G) by crosscutting a 2×4 piece to 20" and ripping it in half.

2. Cut one end of each of the legs (F) at a 38° angle, then cut the other end at the same angle to a finished overall length of 27¼".

Cutting Diagram

4—2 × 4" × 16' Treated Lumber

EXPLODED VIEW

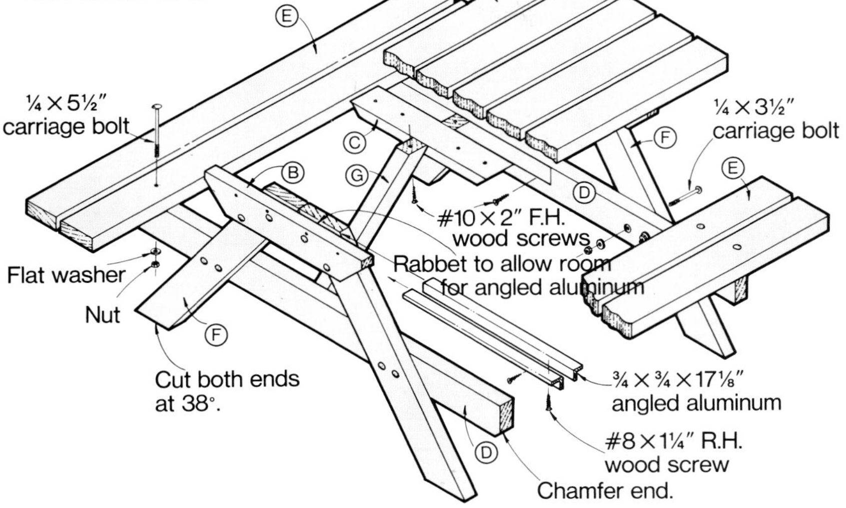
A
E
¼ × 5½″ carriage bolt
¼ × 3½″ carriage bolt
C
F
E
B
G
D
#10 × 2″ F.H. wood screws
Rabbet to allow room for angled aluminum
Flat washer
Nut
F
Cut both ends at 38°.
¾ × ¾ × 17⅛″ angled aluminum
#8 × 1¼″ R.H. wood screw
D
Chamfer end.

Bill of Materials					
Part	**Finished Size**			**Mat.**	**Qty.**
	T	**W**	**L**		
A	1½"	3½"	48"	TL	5
B	1½"	3½"	18"	TL	2
C	1½"	3½"	18"	TL	1
D	1½"	3½"	44"	TL	2
E	1½"	3½"	48"	TL	4
F*	1½"	3½"	27¼"	TL	4
G*	1½"	1½"	16½"	TL	2

*Some parts are cut larger initially, then trimmed to finished size. Please read the instructions before cutting.

Material Key: TL—treated lumber
Supplies: 36—#8X1¼" R.H. wood screws, 8—#10X2" F.H. wood screws, 8—¼"X5½" carriage bolts, 16¼"X3½" carriage bolts, 24—¼" flat washers, 24—¼" nuts, 4 pieces—⅛"X¾"X¾" cut to 17" angled aluminum stock (available at most hardware stores)

3. Cut a ¾" rabbet ¼" deep on the top outside end of each of the legs to allow room for the angled aluminum that's mounted to the supports. (We clamped the legs to the radial arm saw table and used a dado blade to make the rabbet. You can also make the rabbet with a mallet and chisel, or with a router fitted with a straight bit.)

4. Position the two legs on a flat surface as shown in the Leg Marking drawing *below*, flush against a straight 2X4 or a wall. Now, measure up 9" on each leg and mark the location of the top of the seat support (D). Center the seat supports on the legs, then drill ¼" holes and attach them to the legs.

Final assembly

1. Clamp the leg assemblies to the inside of the tabletop supports and drill ¼" holes through the supports and the legs. Fasten the legs to the supports with ¼"X3½" carriage bolts.

2. Clamp the seats (E) to the seat supports (see the End View drawing for positioning). Drill ¼" holes through the supports and seats, then fasten the seats to the supports using ¼"X5½" carriage bolts.

3. To further stabilize the table, cut each end of the braces (G) to 45° and to length to fit between the center brace and seat supports. Drill pilot holes and connect the pieces with #10X2" wood screws.

4. Using a belt sander or sanding block, round-over all sharp edges. Finish, if desired, or let the wood age naturally.

LEG MARKING

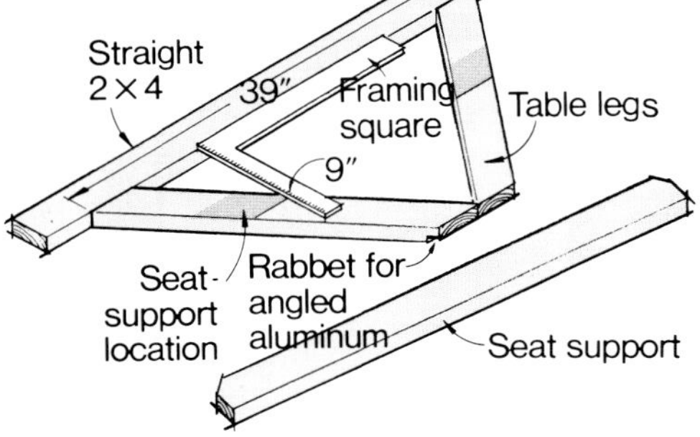
Straight 2×4
39″
Framing square
Table legs
9″
Seat-support location
Rabbet for angled aluminum
Seat support

Project Tool List

Radial-arm saw
  Dado blade or dado set
Portable drill
  Bits: 3/32", 7/64", ¼"
Belt sander

Note: *We built the project using the tools listed. You may be able to substitute other tools or equipment for listed items you don't have. Additional common hand tools and clamps may be required to complete the project.*

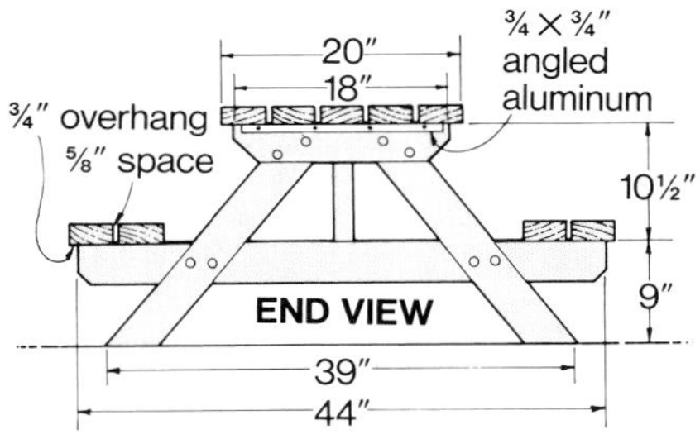
¾ × ¾″ angled aluminum
20″
18″
¾″ overhang
⅝″ space
10½″
9″
END VIEW
39″
44″

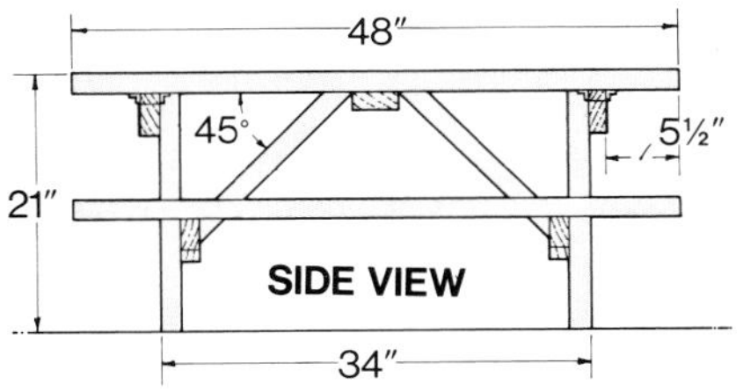
48″
45°
5½″
21″
SIDE VIEW
34″

STUFF FOR KIDS' ROOMS

To make a child's room a fun-filled place, there are a variety of accessories you can construct. The projects in this section range from a friendly clown night-light to a balloon mobile to some toy shelves supported by giraffes.

NIGHT-LIGHT CLOWN

When it's bedtime for little ones, it's worktime for Bozo, our nifty night-light clown shown *opposite*. This delightful scrollsaw project uses a night-light that automatically switches on in the dark. Note in this nighttime photo how the light filters through the outlines of the clown's face and causes his eyes and mouth to glow. Our full-sized pattern lets you build one just like it.

First, prepare the clown cutout

1. Photocopy or trace with carbon paper two copies of the full-sized clown pattern at *right*. Put one pattern copy aside for now.

2. Apply double-faced tape to cover the back of the pattern, and adhere it to a piece of ⅛"-thick craft plywood that measures 4x7". (You can find thin plywood at hobby and crafts shops or use ⅛"-thick tempered hardboard.) The tape holds the pattern on the wood surface, and reduces chip-out when sawing.

3. Chuck a ½" bit (we used a brad-point bit) in your drill press, back the workpiece with scrap, and drill the ½" holes in the bow tie and hat. Drill ⅛" start holes for the saw blade in the eyes and mouth. Switch to a ⅝" bit and drill the nose hole. You'll cut out the incomplete circles with a scrollsaw later.

4. Cut an auxiliary top (we used cardboard) for your scrollsaw, and tape it to the tabletop. Poke or drill a 1⁄16" hole through it for the blade. This will keep the small parts from falling through the table's slot. Now, scrollsaw the eyes and mouth openings as shown at *far right* by threading the saw blade through the ⅛" holes you drilled in these areas.

5. Next, scrollsaw the clown parts to shape, including the incomplete circles in the hat. Lightly sand the bottom of each part. Peel off the pattern and tape,

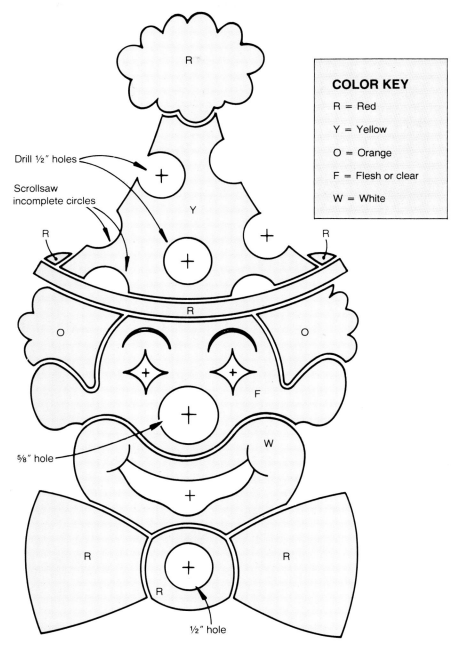

Drill ½" holes

Scrollsaw incomplete circles

⅝" hole

½" hole

FULL– SIZED PATTERN

and wipe off any tape residue with lacquer thinner.

Next, paint the clown

1. Cover a work board (plywood or cardboard) with double-faced tape. Place the clown parts on the tape, face-side up just as you *continued*

NIGHT-LIGHT CLOWN
continued

would view them in the finished project. (We did not paint the face piece. Instead, we applied three coats of clear lacquer to it for a natural flesh color. We outlined the eyes, ears, and eyebrows with black paint.)

2. Spray the other clown parts with a light coat of primer/sealer paint. On hardboard, seal with sanding sealer.

3. Next, brush-paint the parts. You may want to experiment on the paper pattern with crayons or felt markers to visualize what parts to paint, or to select your own color scheme. (For paint, we used Pactra Odds 'n' Ends, a brand of nontoxic fast-drying enamel paints available at True Value stores. See the pattern for our color choices.) Paint the edges on each piece also.

Assemble the clown and night-light

1. Tape your second copy of the clown pattern to the underside of a sheet of ⅛"-thick acrylic measuring 5X7". (You can buy acrylic at hardware stores and home centers).

2. Begin assembling the clown by first applying one or two drops of adhesive to the back of the flesh-colored face piece. (We used Hot Stuff-Super T, a form of cyanoacrylate [super-glue] adhesive and sprayed it with Hot Stuff accelerator to speed the curing of the glue. A general purpose cement such as Duco or epoxy also works.) Position the part on the acrylic directly over the pattern's face. (We sprayed the glue from the side again with accelerator.) Now, glue the other parts in position one by one, using a paper clip to gauge the spacing between the parts as shown at *top right.*

3. To undercut the acrylic, angle the table on your scrollsaw to 15° from horizontal as shown on the Undercutting Detail drawing *above.* Next, place the assembled clown

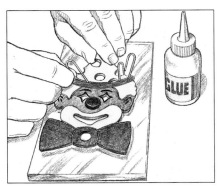

on the saw table face up. Start cutting the acrylic following the clown's shape. Keep the part of the clown being sawed on the downhill side of the blade, as shown *below bottom,* letting the bottom edge of the clown guide the blade as you undercut the acrylic. (We found the acrylic cuts better when we fed the work slowly so the blade did not heat up and melt the acrylic.)

Note: *For the night-light, we used Novo Light model NL 301 available at True Value hardware stores. It has a photoelectric eye that*

UNDERCUTTING DETAIL

Saw blade

Clown face

Acrylic

Angle saw table 15°

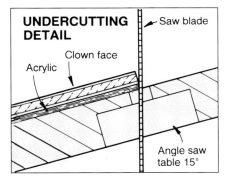

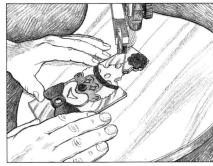

automatically turns on the light when darkness sets in. It also features a rectangular-shaped plastic cover with a flat, straight front surface that's ideal for mounting the clown assembly to.

4. To prevent light from the unit reflecting into the photoelectric eye (and causing the light to flicker on and off at high speed), cover the backside of the bow tie with black electrical tape where shown on the Exploded View drawing *opposite.*

5. To join the clown and light assembly, place the night-light in a wall receptacle. Hold the clown in front of the light, center the hole in the bow tie over the photoelectric eye, and center the face vertically. Use masking tape to hold it in place. Next, remove the assembly from the receptacle and place it on a flat surface, clown face down. Now, apply several fillets of glue along the edge of the night-light cover where it meets the acrylic as shown *below.* Spray the glue with accelerator to speed its curing.

6. Apply a drop of adhesive to the end of a ½" screw hole button Now, center it in the nose hole.

7. If necessary, touch up any of the outside edges of the clown you may have scraped with the saw when cutting the acrylic. Use the matching color of paint.

8. Place the night-light in an electrical receptacle. You can test the light by temporarily covering the light sensor in the bow tie hole.

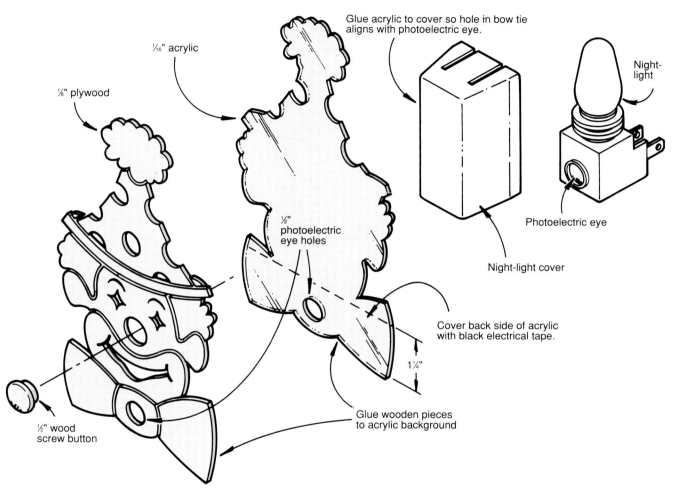

Glue acrylic to cover so hole in bow tie aligns with photoelectric eye.

1⁄16" acrylic

1⁄8" plywood

Night-light

Photoelectric eye

Night-light cover

1⁄2" photoelectric eye holes

Cover back side of acrylic with black electrical tape.

1 1⁄4"

Glue wooden pieces to acrylic background

1⁄2" wood screw button

Buying Guide
• **1⁄8" plywood.** Poplar, 3-ply, 1⁄8x9 1⁄4x11 3⁄8" sheet. Catalog no. 7546. For current price, contact Meisel Hardware Specialties, P.O. Box 70, Mound, MN 55634-0070.
• **Cyanoacrylate adhesive.** "Hot Stuff-Super T," 2-oz. bottle gap-filling adhesive. Catalog no. 08X31. "Hot Shot" accelerator, 3 oz. spray bottle. Catalog no. 08X41. For

current prices, contact Woodcraft, 41 Atlantic Ave., P.O. Box 4000, Woburn, MA 01888. Phone 800-225-1153.

Supplies
Double-faced tape, masking tape, primer paint, enamel paints, spray lacquer, 1⁄8"-thick acrylic, paper clips, 1—1⁄2" screw hole button.

Project Tool List
Scrollsaw
Drill press
    Bits: 1⁄8", 1⁄2", 5⁄8"

Note: We built the project using the tools listed. You may be able to substitute other tools or equipment for listed items you don't have. Additional common hand tools and clamps may be required to complete the project.

ARK-ED DOORWAY

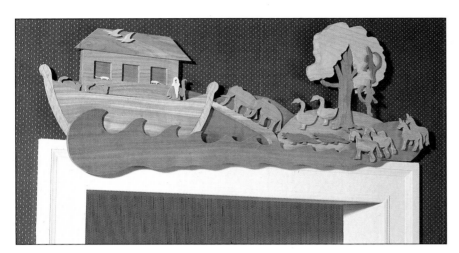

"T_here was green alligators and long-neck geese."_ **And humpty-back camels and some chimpanzees. Sorry, there wasn't room for all of Mother Earth's wildlife on our ark, but we did squeeze in the critters mentioned in the Irish Rover's classic song,** _The Unicorn_ **. This over-the-door project focuses attention on a neglected room area, and seems perfect for a child's room—or perhaps a church school classroom.**

First, prepare the full-sized patterns

1. Enlarge the nine gridded patterns on _page 37_ by taping 8½×11" sheets of paper end to end to form required lengths. Starting at one corner, draw 1" squares across the surface of each sheet.

2. Using the gridded patterns as guides, draw each pattern outline on a gridded form. (When enlarging gridded patterns, we first plot the points where the pattern lines cross the grid lines, and then draw lines to connect the points.)

3. Copy the full-sized patterns on _page 36_. With scissors, cut out all patterns, leaving a ½" margin around the borders.

4. Prepare ¼" stock for these parts: background layer (A, B),

6×37" and 3×10"; goose hill (C), 5×15", boat cabin (D), 6×9"; wave (E), 6×32"; roof (F), 2×11"; unicorn hill (G), 4×10"; tree trunk (H), 9×5"; and the stem (I) and stern (J). Next, cut the hull (K) and ramp (L) from ½×5×14" stock; the tree canopy (M) from ¾×7×9" stock. Use ¼" stock for Noah, the animals, and birds; ⅛" stock for both rats and Noah's beard and hair. Now, glue and edge-join the two background pieces where instructed on the pattern, and clamp until the glue dries.

**Note:** We suggest you cut the parts from at least three different wood species for contrast. For example, we cut the animals from basswood, cherry, walnut, mahogany, and oak. For the ark we used cherry, oak, and walnut. Walnut also makes up the background and the wave.

5. Sand the best face on each piece with 150-grit sandpaper. Apply a misting of spray adhesive to the back of each pattern, and adhere them to the pieces you just sanded. To speed cutting out the animals, stack two pieces of stock face to face with double-faced tape, and adhere the patterns to the top piece.

6. Chuck a keyhole or dovetail bit in your table-mounted router,

and set the bit height. See the Router Setup drawing _opposite_ for details on how to adjust your router table to cut the keyhole slots in the back face of the background. Rout the keyhole slots.

You're ready to scrollsaw

1. Scrollsaw all of the pieces except the ramp. (We used a #5 blade.) Drill ¼"-start holes through the cabin windows, and thread your scrollsaw blade through each hole. For a good fit, cut out the tree canopy first, and use it to scribe the mating joints on the tree branches.

2. For a good joint between the hull and the stem and stern, scribe the hull outline on the mating edge of both pieces, and then cut out the stem and stern.

3. Remove the patterns. Dry-fit the parts except the animals, and adjust where necessary to fit.

Start assembling the ark

1. Cover your work surface with waxed paper, and place the background piece on top of it. Spread a light layer of glue on the cabin's back, position it on your background, and clamp to hold the piece in place. Use the Exploded View drawing _opposite_ and the dashed lines on the patterns to position the pieces. Remove glue squeeze-out with a damp cloth.

2. Apply glue to the ends of the tree limbs; center the canopy around the limbs and hold in place with rubber bands until the glue dries. Now, glue the stem and stern to the hull and clamp.

3. Glue the goose hill and the assembled ark hull to the background. Glue the roof to the cabin. Clamp. After the glue dries, adhere the tree and unicorn hill to the front of the goose hill. Scrollsaw the ramp, trim it to fit where shown, and glue it in place. Clamp.

4. Glue on the animals. To avoid glue smears, apply glue prudently. (Hotmelt adhesive also works.)

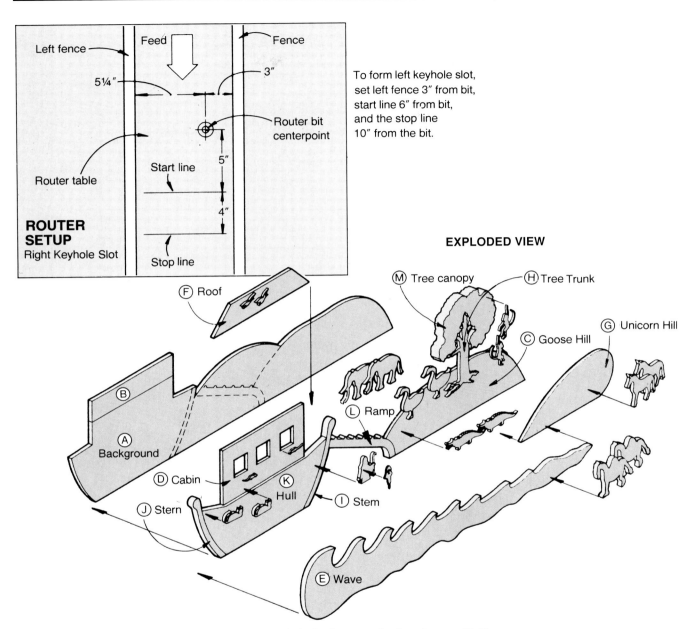

ROUTER SETUP
Right Keyhole Slot

Left fence

Feed

Fence

5¼"

3"

Router bit centerpoint

Start line

5"

4"

Stop line

Router table

To form left keyhole slot, set left fence 3″ from bit, start line 6″ from bit, and the stop line 10″ from the bit.

EXPLODED VIEW

Ⓜ Tree canopy

Ⓗ Tree Trunk

Ⓕ Roof

Ⓒ Goose Hill

Ⓖ Unicorn Hill

Ⓑ

Ⓐ Background

Ⓛ Ramp

Ⓓ Cabin

Ⓚ Hull

Ⓘ Stem

Ⓙ Stern

Ⓔ Wave

5. Apply the finish of your choice. (We left ours unfinished; however, you may want to seal the woods with a clear spray-on lacquer.)

6. To mount the ark to the wall, hold it in position over the door and scribe a faint mark along the stem end. Measure in 4" from the mark you just made and 3" up from the top of your door frame. Mark this spot. From that centerpoint, sure over 22" to locate the second screw-hole centerpoint. Drill ⅛" pilot holes at these points, and then drive a #8x1½" flathead wood screw

into each hole, leaving the heads extended from the wall about ¼". Place the plaque over the screws, and center it by sliding it from side to side. Adjust screw depth if necessary for fit.

Supplies
Waxed paper, #8x1½" flathead wood screws, finish.

Project Tool List
Tablesaw
Scrollsaw
Router
    Dovetail or keyhole bit

Drill press
    Bits: ⁵⁄₆₄", ⅛", ¼"
Finishing sander

Note: *We built the project using the tools listed. You may be able to substitute other tools or equipment for listed items you don't have. Additional common hand tools and clamps may be required to complete the project.*

ARK-ED DOORWAY
continued

FULL-SIZED PATTERNS

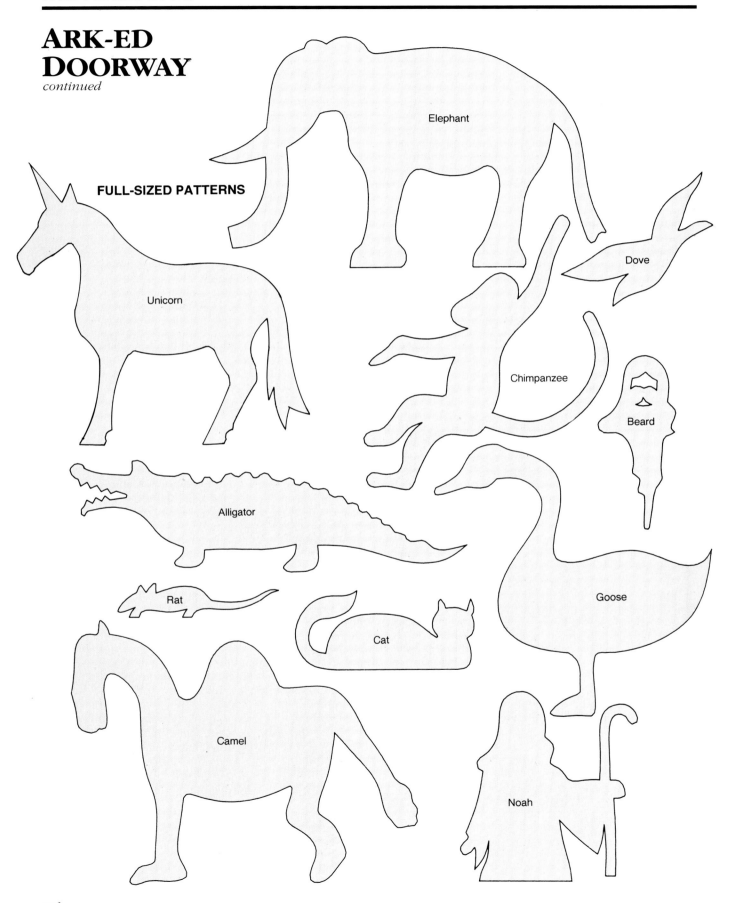

Elephant

Dove

Unicorn

Chimpanzee

Beard

Alligator

Goose

Rat

Cat

Camel

Noah

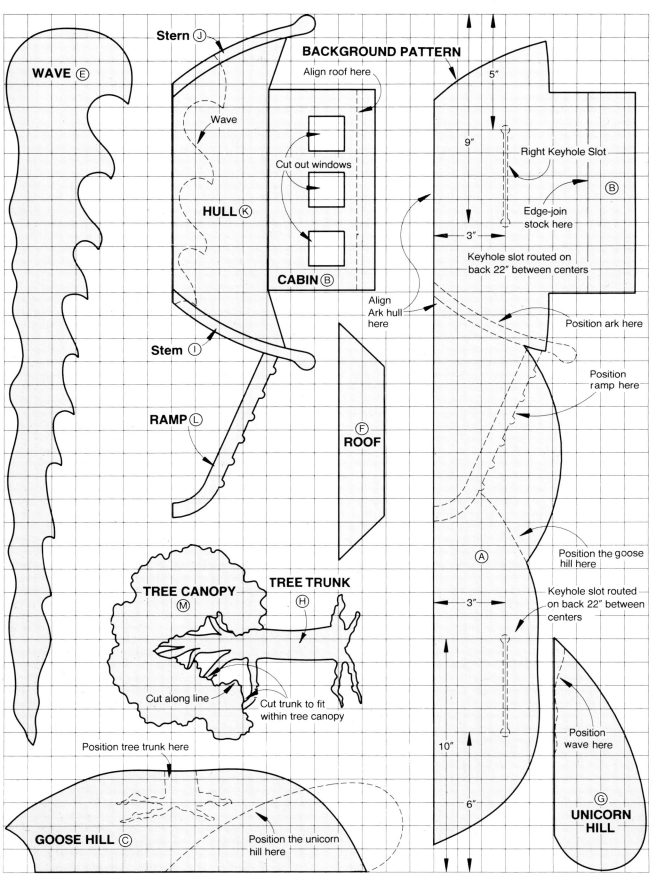

WAVE (E)

Stern (J)

Wave

HULL (K)

Stem (I)

RAMP (L)

BACKGROUND PATTERN

Align roof here

Cut out windows

CABIN (B)

5″

9″

Right Keyhole Slot

Edge-join stock here

3″

(B)

Keyhole slot routed on back 22″ between centers

Align Ark hull here

Position ark here

Position ramp here

(F)
ROOF

Position the goose hill here

(A)

3″

Keyhole slot routed on back 22″ between centers

TREE CANOPY
(M)

TREE TRUNK
(H)

Cut along line

Cut trunk to fit within tree canopy

Position tree trunk here

10″

Position wave here

6″

(G)
UNICORN HILL

GOOSE HILL (C)

Position the unicorn hill here

GRIDDED PATTERNS 1 square = 1″

WALL-HUNG GAME CABINET

An evening of fun can be as close as the rec room with this two-in-one game center. Let the kids toss the rings, and later the adults can throw a few darts. Whether you toss darts or rings, you'll appreciate keeping tally with the easy to use and clean scoreboard inside the right door.

Start with the frame

1. Cut the frame top and bottom (A) and the sides (B) to the dimensions listed in the Bill of Materials *opposite*. (We used beech for the cabinet carcase and doors.)

2. Cut a ¾" rabbet ⅜" deep across each end of the side pieces (see the Exploded View drawing *opposite* for additional details).

3. Mark the hinge-mortise locations on both side pieces (B) where shown on the Exploded View drawing. Cut the hinge recesses. (After marking the locations, we mounted a ¾" dado blade to our tablesaw, and raised the dado blade ³⁄₃₂" above the saw table. We then attached an extension to our miter gauge for extra support, and test-cut a hinge mortise in scrap material to verify the correct depth before cutting the mortises.)

4. Glue and clamp the four frame pieces (A, B). Square the assembly. Remove glue squeeze-out with a damp cloth.

5. Rout a ¼" rabbet ⅜" deep along the back inside edge of the frame assembly. Square the rounded corners with a sharp chisel.

6. Measure the rabbeted opening. Cut the back (C) to fit from ¼" plywood stock.

7. Mark the locations, and drill a pair of ⁵⁄₁₆" holes ⁵⁄₁₆" deep in the front edge of the top piece (A) for the round magnetic catches.

Prepare the doors and rout the decorative groove

1. Rip and crosscut the two doors (D) to size from ¾"-thick beech stock. (For economy and stability, we edge-joined pieces of narrower stock to achieve the 11½" width.)

2. Clamp both doors to your benchtop with the top and bottom edges flush in the configuration shown on the Doors drawing on *page 40*. Using trammel points, mark a 37"-radius arc across the door tops (see the Doors drawing).

3. Cut the tops to shape on a band-saw, cutting just outside the marked line. Now, sand to the line to remove the saw marks.

4. To rout the decorative groove in the door fronts, first make a full-sized template pattern using the Door Panel Template drawing on *page 41*. Next, transfer this pattern to a piece of ½" plywood, and then cut and sand the template to shape.

5. Position the template on a door front and trace its location onto the door with a pencil. Remove the template, and place two strips of double-faced tape on the template back. Now, adhere the template to the door where previously marked.

6. Mount a ¼" straight bit and ½" guide bushing to your router and adjust it as shown on the Groove Detail accompanying the Exploded View drawing and the drawing *opposite*. Now, hold the router's guide bushing against the edge of the ½"-thick template, and carefully rout the ⅛" groove around the edge of the template. For best results, rout counterclockwise.

7. Remove the template from the door front (we used a wooden wedge). If you find the templates hard to remove, a splash of lacquer thinner under the template will help dissolve the tape's adhesive. Now, flip the template over, and

EXPLODED VIEW

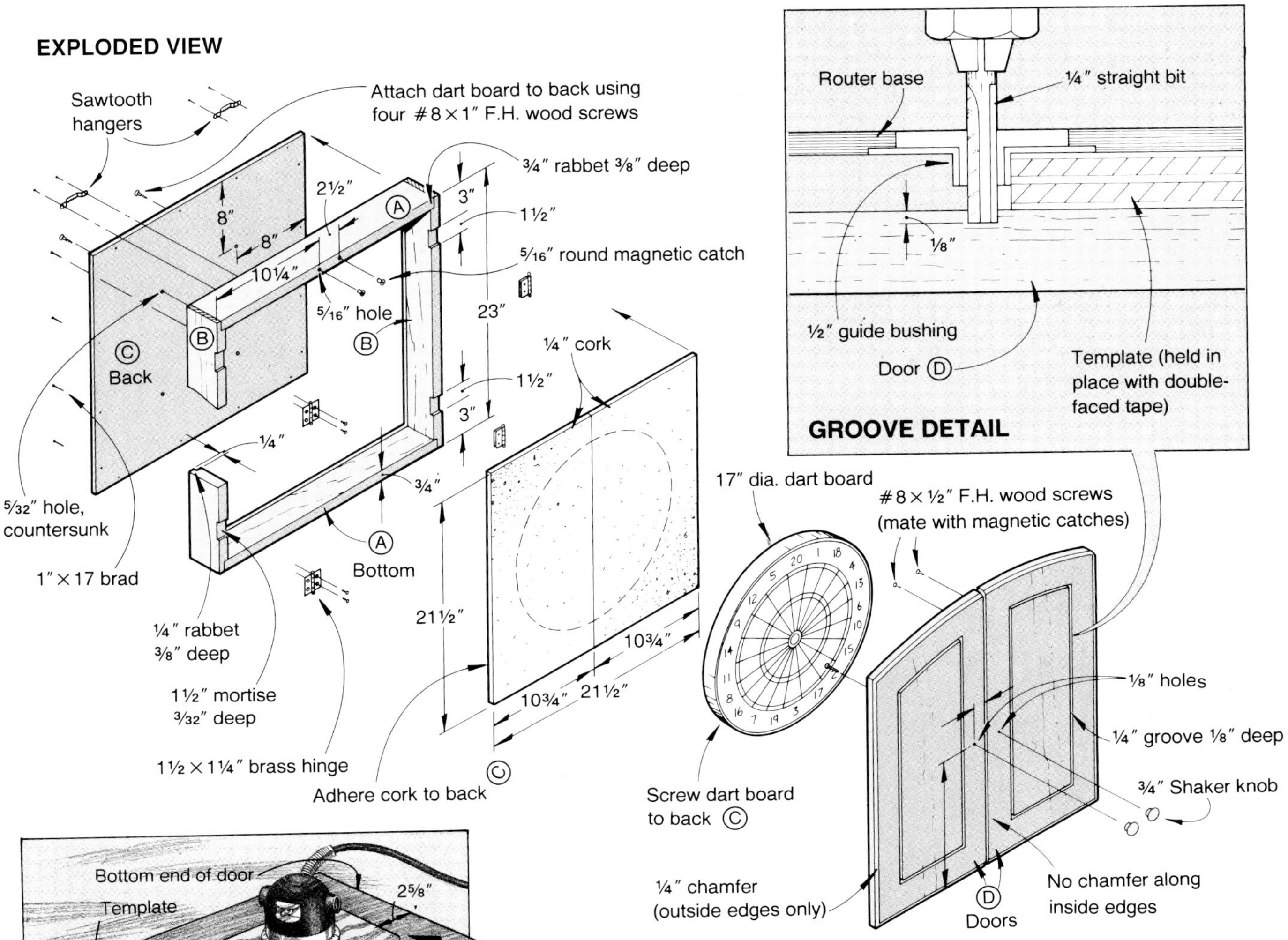

Sawtooth hangers
Attach dart board to back using four #8 × 1″ F.H. wood screws
3/4″ rabbet 3/8″ deep
2 1/2″
8″
8″
10 1/4″
3″
1 1/2″
5/16″ round magnetic catch
5/16″ hole
23″
Ⓐ
Ⓑ
Ⓑ
Ⓒ Back
1/4″ cork
1 1/2″
3″
1/4″
3/4″
5/32″ hole, countersunk
Ⓐ Bottom
1″ × 17 brad
1/4″ rabbet 3/8″ deep
21 1/2″
10 3/4″
1 1/2″ mortise 3/32″ deep
10 3/4″
21 1/2″
1 1/2 × 1 1/4″ brass hinge
Adhere cork to back Ⓒ
17″ dia. dart board
#8 × 1/2″ F.H. wood screws (mate with magnetic catches)
1/8″ holes
1/4″ groove 1/8″ deep
3/4″ Shaker knob
Screw dart board to back Ⓒ
1/4″ chamfer (outside edges only)
Ⓓ Doors
No chamfer along inside edges
Router base
1/4″ straight bit
1/8″
1/2″ guide bushing
Door Ⓓ
Template (held in place with double-faced tape)
GROOVE DETAIL

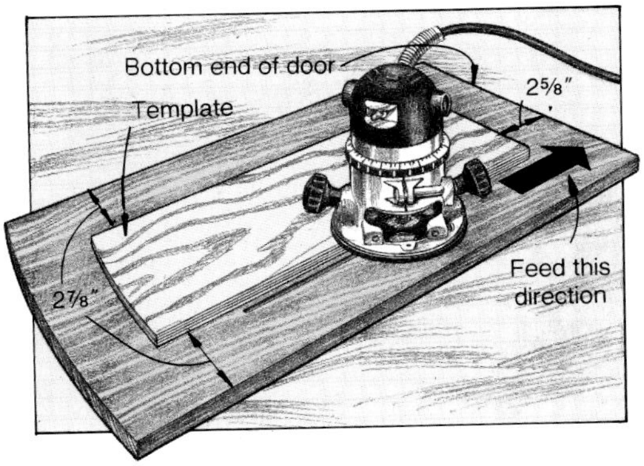

Bottom end of door
Template
2 5/8″
2 7/8″
Feed this direction

repeat the process in steps 5 and 6 to rout the groove in the front face of the second door.

8. Switch bits, and rout a ¼" chamfer along the edges of each door. *Do not* chamfer the mating edges.

9. Using the dimensions on the Doors drawing, mark the locations, and drill 1/16" pilot holes ½" deep in the back side of the left-hand door for the square-bend screw hooks. Be careful not to drill through the door. Sand the door to remove the pencil marks. Next, mark the knob locations where shown on the Exploded View drawing. Drill a ⅛" mounting screw hole through the door for each knob.

Add cork for darts that miss the mark

1. Fit the back piece (C) into the rabbeted opening of the carcase and tape it in place.

2. Cut pieces of ⅛"- or ¼"-thick decorative cork to fit neatly inside the frame assembly opening and onto the front face of the cabinet back. (Working carefully, we cut our cork with a sharp utility knife and straightedge.)

3. Adhere the cork to the plywood back with double-faced tape, hotmelt adhesive, or glue.

continued

Bill of Materials

Part	Finished Size T	W	L	Mat.	Qty.
A top, bottom	¾"	3"	22¼"	B	2
B side	¾"	3"	23"	B	2
C back	¼"	22¼"	22¼"	P	1
D doors	¾"	11½"	25"	B	2
E dart holder	¾"	1"	8½"	B	1
F score board	¼"	8½"	14½"	H	1

Material Key: B–beech, P–plywood, H–hardboard

Supplies: 17"-dia. dart board, 1"X17 brads, two pair of 1½X1¼" brass broad hinges (Stanley CD5302), 13—1½"-long square-bend screw hooks (Stanley 8465-910), ¼" fine-textured cork, 2—⅜"-round magnetic catches and #8X½" flathead wood screws, 2—sawtooth hangers, ¾" Shaker knobs, 2—#8X1½" flathead brass wood screws, 6—finish (counter-sunk) washers, #8X¾" brass wood screws, #8X1" flathead wood screws, stain, finish, green chalkboard paint, white vinyl tape, ¾" Zipatone vinyl numerals, rubber jar rings.

WALL-HUNG GAME CABINET

continued

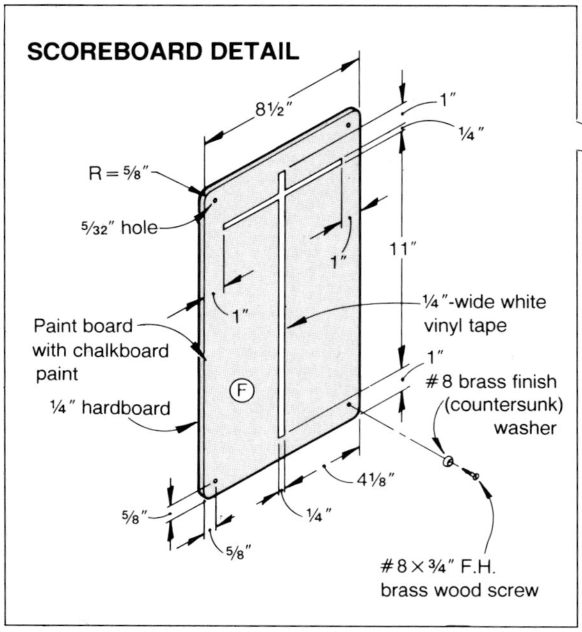
SCOREBOARD DETAIL
8½"
1"
¼"
R = ⅝"
5/32" hole
1"
11"
1"
¼"-wide white vinyl tape
Paint board with chalkboard paint
1"
#8 brass finish (countersunk) washer
F
¼" hardboard
4⅛"
⅝"
¼"
⅝"
#8 × ¾" F.H. brass wood screw

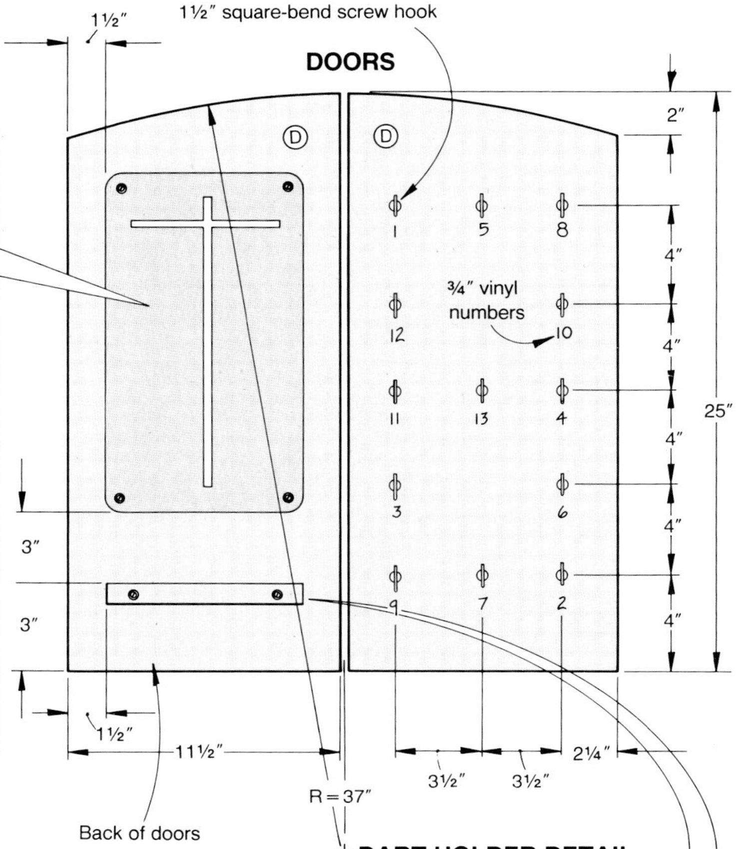
1½"
1½" square-bend screw hook
DOORS
D
D
2"
1
5
8
4"
¾" vinyl numbers
12
10
4"
11
13
4
25"
4"
3
6
4"
3"
9
7
2
4"
3"
1½"
11½"
3½"
3½"
2¼"
R = 37"
Back of doors

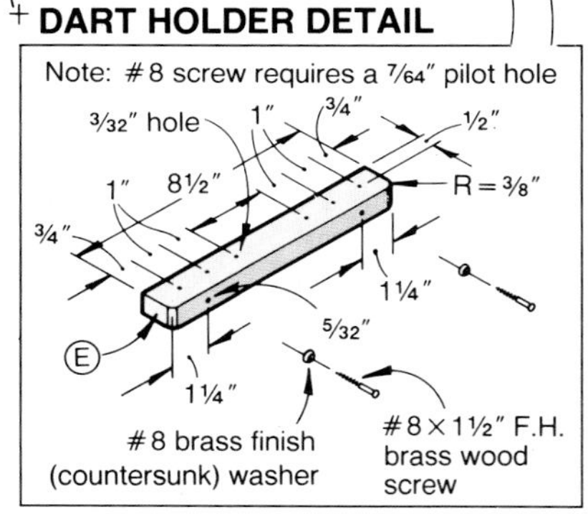
DART HOLDER DETAIL
Note: #8 screw requires a 7/64" pilot hole
3/32" hole
1"
¾"
½"
1"
8½"
R = ⅜"
¾"
1¼"
5/32"
E
1¼"
#8 brass finish (countersunk) washer
#8 × 1½" F.H. brass wood screw

4. Using the Exploded View drawing for reference, mark the four hole locations for fastening the dartboard to the plywood. Working from the back side, drill and countersink the four 5/32" screw holes. Center the dart board in the frame. Now, screw the back to the dart board, and then remove it from the assembly. (We purchased our ½X17" dart board with metal dividers and 6 brass darts at K Mart.)

Add the dart holder and scoreboard

1. Using the dimensions on the Dart Holder detail at *right*, cut the holder (E) to size. Saw or sand ⅜" radius on the two front corners.

2. Using the same drawing for reference, mark the location, and drill a pair of 5/32" mounting hole through the holder edge and six 3/32" holes for the darts.

3. Carefully position and then clamp the dart holder to the inside of the right-hand door. Next, using the previously drilled mounting holes in the holder as guides, drill a pair of 7/64" pilot holes ⅜" deep into the door back.

4. Cut the scoreboard (F) to size from ¼" hardboard. Mark a ⅝" radius at each corner. Cut to shape.

5. Mark the locations, and drill all four mounting holes through the scoreboard. Clamp the scoreboard to the back of the right-hand door. Drill the pilot holes into the inside face of the door but do not attach the scoreboard yet.

Now, sand, finish, and add the hardware

1. Finish-sand the frame, doors, scoreboard, and dart holder. Finish as desired. (We applied two coats of water-based sanding sealer, and sanded lightly after each coat. Next, we applied three coats of water-based satin lacquer, and then sanded with 220-grit sandpaper.)

2. Paint the scoreboard with green chalkboard paint. (We sprayed four light coats to build up the paint surface, and sanded lightly between coats to keep the surface smooth.) After the paint dries, cut two ¼"-wide strips of white vinyl tape and adhere them to the front face where shown on the Scoreboard detail. Attach the

DOOR PANEL ROUTING TEMPLATE

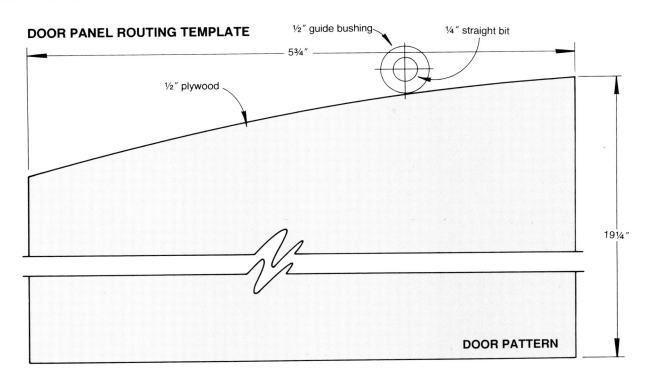

½" guide bushing

¼" straight bit

5¾"

½" plywood

19¼"

DOOR PATTERN

scoreboard to the right door with #8 brass finish washers and #8X¾" flathead brass screws. Attach dart holder.

3. Apply self-adhering ¾"-high vinyl numbers to the inside face of the left door in the configuration shown on the Doors drawing. (We used Zippy-Sign ¾" Helvetica numerals by Zipatone; ask for them at art and crafts-supply stores.)

4. Fit the back into the rabbeted frame opening, and secure it to the frame with 1"X17 brads. Attach sawtooth hangers to the back.

5. Screw the square-bend screw hooks into the previously drilled

holes in the left door. Attach a knob to the front of each door.

6. Using spring clamps, clamp a long straight board to the dart board bottom piece (A) where shown in the drawing at *left* to align the doors and cabinet. Using books or scrap pieces of wood as spacers, raise the doors so the top surface of the door lays flush with the bottom surface of the mortise. Now, align the door bottoms flush against this guide board.

7. Attach the hinges in the frame mortises, and then screw them to the door backs.

8. Insert both round magnetic catches in the holes in the frame top. Next, opposite these magnets, drive #8X½" flathead wood screws into the inside face of each door to act as strike plates.

9. Mount the cabinet so the bull's eye center measures 68" from the floor. The throwing or hockey line should be 93¼" in front and parallel to the face of the dart board. For the ring-toss game, purchase a box of rubber rings used on quart canning jars.

Project Tool List

Tablesaw
    Dado blade or dado set
Bandsaw
Drill press
    Bits: ¹⁄₁₆", ³⁄₃₂", ⁷⁄₆₄", ⅛", ⁵⁄₃₂", ⁵⁄₁₆"
Router
    Bits: ¼" straight, chamfer
    ½" guide brushing
Finishing sander

Note: *We built the project using the tools listed. You may be able to substitute other tools or equipment for listed items you don't have. Additional common hand tools and clamps may be required to complete the project.*

AN AQUATIC CLOTHES TREE FOR YOUNGSTERS

Thar she blows! 'Tis the finest child's clothes tree on land or sea, complete with playful dolphins for hooks. Aye, it would take a lifetime of sailing the seven seas to find another nearly this fine. What's more, even a landlubber can craft this one as easily as Flipper can leap through a hoop.

Note: *You'll need a piece of ⅛" thick stock 3×36" for the flippers on our aquatic mammals. Plane or resaw thicker stock to size.*

1. Cut eight ¾×6× 9" hardwood boards, and then crosscut a length of 1½×1½" stock to 42". (We chose birch.) Fasten the 6×9" boards together into stacks of four with double-faced tape, aligning the edges. With spray adhesive, attach a photocopy of the dolphin pattern, *opposite,* to the top of one stack and the whale pattern to the other.

2. Cut out the dolphins and whales with a bandsaw. *(Scrollsawers: Since scrollsaws won't handle a three-inch stack, make an extra copy of each pattern, tape your boards together in pairs, and cut out the whales and dolphins two at a time.* Cut eight whale flippers and eight dolphin flippers from ⅛" stock.

3. Without separating the cutouts, sand all edges with a drum sander in a drill press, or by hand where the drum won't reach. Mark the location of the dowel holes where shown on the patterns, and then separate the cut pieces. Mark the dowel-hole locations

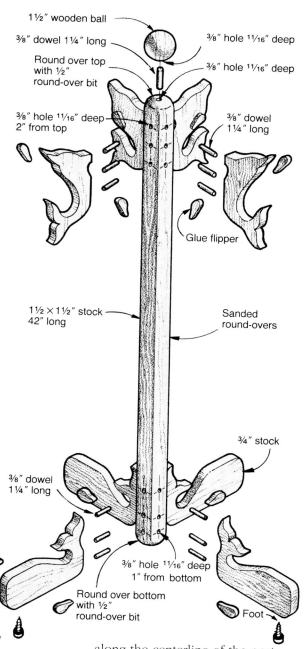

1½" wooden ball

⅜" dowel 1¼" long

Round over top with ½" round-over bit

⅜" hole ¹¹⁄₁₆" deep

⅜" hole ¹¹⁄₁₆" deep

⅜" hole ¹¹⁄₁₆" deep 2" from top

⅜" dowel 1¼" long

Glue flipper

1½ × 1½" stock 42" long

Sanded round-overs

¾" stock

⅜" dowel 1¼" long

⅜" hole ¹¹⁄₁₆" deep 1" from bottom

Round over bottom with ½" round-over bit

Foot

along the centerline of the post where shown, transferring the spacing from the cutouts.

4. Center the edge holes on the cutouts with a doweling jig. Then, drill the ⅜" dowel holes ¹¹⁄₁₆" deep with a brad-point bit.

5. For the upright post, place a fence on your drill-press table to center the bit on the work. Then, using a stop-block and clamp, bore the lower hole on each face. Continue by moving the block and drilling each face at each of the remaining five positions. Rout ½" round-overs along the top and bottom of the post with a table-mounted router.

6. Then, grip a 1½"-diameter wooden ball with a handscrew clamp, and drill a ⅜" dowel hole ¹¹⁄₁₆" deep in it with the drill press. Center a like-sized dowel hole on top of the post.

7. Sand all pieces. Glue the flippers on, and then paint the dolphins and whales. (We used Ceramcoat colors indicated on the patterns.) Assemble with dowels and glue. Apply a clear finish, and add rubber feet.

Project Tool List
Tablesaw
Bandsaw or scrollsaw
Portable drill
Drill press
    ⅜" bit
Drum sander
Router
    Router table
    ½" round-over bit
Finishing sander

Note: We built the project using the tools listed. You may be able to substitute other tools or equipment for listed items you don't have. Additional common hand tools and clamps may be required to complete the project.

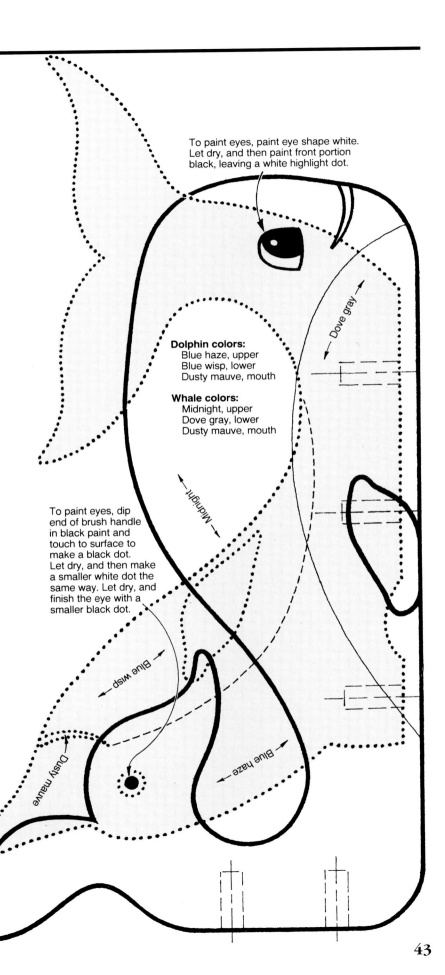

To paint eyes, paint eye shape white. Let dry, and then paint front portion black, leaving a white highlight dot.

Dolphin colors:
Blue haze, upper
Blue wisp, lower
Dusty mauve, mouth

Whale colors:
Midnight, upper
Dove gray, lower
Dusty mauve, mouth

To paint eyes, dip end of brush handle in black paint and touch to surface to make a black dot. Let dry, and then make a smaller white dot the same way. Let dry, and finish the eye with a smaller black dot.

Dove gray

Midnight

Blue wisp

Dusty mauve

Blue haze

TOY DISPLAY SHELF

Toy-box treasures in miniature enrich this nostalgic wall decoration, a perfect country accent for a child's room.

1. Joint or saw one edge of a length of 2x4 to remove the rounded edges, and cut an 8"-1ong piece for the base. Make a copy of the full-sized pattern, *opposite,* and adhere the base portion to the 2x4 piece with spray adhesive or trace the outline with carbon paper. Align the top of the pattern with the jointed edge.

2. Next cut a 5½" length of knot-free 1x6, and rip a ¾" strip from one edge. Also, cut a 1⅜x4" piece of ¼" stock (here we used lattice molding).

3. Transfer the bear/wagon pattern to the 1x6 piece, aligning the front of the wagon with one end of the stock. Transfer the arm pattern onto the ¼" stock.

4. Drill a 1/16" hole ½" deep for the wagon handle where shown on the pattern. Then, scrollsaw or bandsaw the bear/wagon, the arm, and the base. Cut three ¾" blocks from the ¾x¾" strip.

5. Sand a flat spot about ½" in diameter on a 1¼"-diameter wooden ball. Sand all parts and trace the painting lines to them.

6. Paint the parts with acrylic colors before assembling, following the color scheme shown in the photograph *above right.* Apply thinned walnut stain to the edges of the base and bear/wagon part to give an aged look. Paint the wheels with thinned raw umber.

7. Draw the dashed lines on the bear's face, his eyes, and his nose with a fine, black, nylon-tipped pen. Rub cosmetic blush on his cheeks for the rosy highlights, and paint the block and base letters with a ⅛" flat brush.

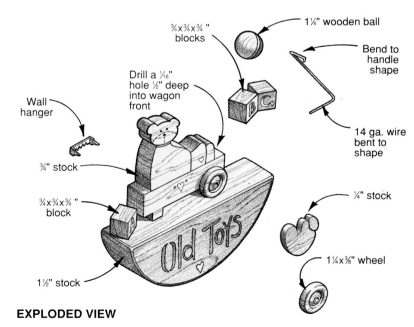

¾x¾x¾ " blocks

1¼" wooden ball

Drill a 1/16" hole ½" deep into wagon front

Bend to handle shape

Wall hanger

14 ga. wire bent to shape

¾" stock

¾x¾x¾ " block

¼" stock

1½" stock

1¼x⅜" wheel

EXPLODED VIEW

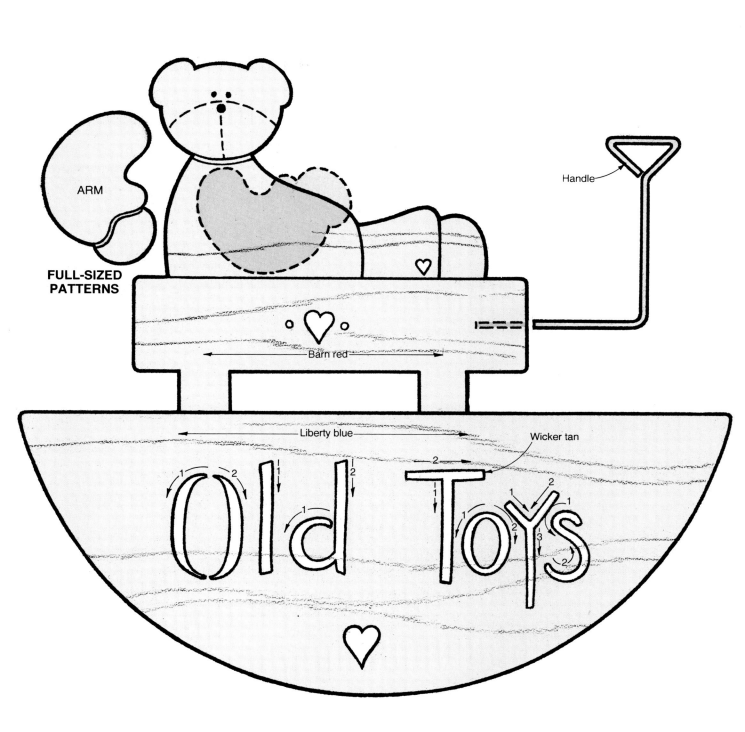

FULL-SIZED PATTERNS

ARM

Handle

Barn red

Liberty blue

Wicker tan

Old Toys

8. Form the wagon handle from a 6" length of soft 14-gauge wire, such as baling wire. Epoxy the handle into the hole and bend it toward the bear. Using hotmelt adhesive, assemble the parts where shown in the drawing.

Project Tool List
Tablesaw
Bandsaw or scrollsaw
Portable drill
  ⅟₁₆" bit
Disc sander
Finishing sander

Note: We built the project using the tools listed. You may be able to substitute other tools or equipment for listed items you don't have. Additional common hand tools and clamps may be required to complete the project.

HIGH-FLYING BALLOON MOBILE

To "air" is human, to turn these balloons, divine. We've turned several, and developed a helpful clamping jig to simplify the laminating process. We also used an auxiliary faceplate to turn the basket. Even after you've completed this project, you'll find these two shop aids helpful.

Note: The instructions explain how to make the checkered-pattern balloon. Repeat the lamination process aligning the pieces differently to form the top two balloons as in the photo at right.

First, form each layer with miter-cut pieces

1. Cut a piece of ¾" walnut and a piece of ¾" maple to 1½x40".

2. Set the miter gauge on your tablesaw 30° from center, and cut 15 pieces of each species to the shape shown on the block detail *opposite.* (We attached a wooden auxiliary fence to our miter gauge, and then clamped a stop to the fence for consistent lengths. We test-cut six scrap pieces to verify the angle.)

3. Alternate and clamp pieces of walnut and maple, as shown on the drawing *opposite.* The setup shown helps keep the top and bottom surfaces flush. Use a rubber band to hold the pieces. Then, switch to a band clamp to hold the pieces firmly together. (We placed waxed paper between the particleboard discs and the lamination to prevent them from bonding.) Repeat for each of the five remaining layers.

4. If necessary to flatten surfaces, lightly sand the top and bottom surfaces of each layer (we did this on a stationary sander).

Glue and align the individual laminated layers, and then tighten the ⅜" nut to clamp the layers together.

The clamping jib helps laminate the layers

1. Spread glue on the mating surfaces. Carefully align the joint lines, and clamp the layers together, using the clamping device as shown *above*.

2. From ¾" stock, cut four maple discs 4⅛" in diameter. Drill a ¹⁄₁₆" hole centered in each disc. Glue and clamp two discs centered on the top and two centered on the bottom of the lamination.

Let's move to the lathe and have some fun

1. Transfer the balloon template pattern shown at *right* to poster board. Cut the template to shape with an X-acto knife.

2. Mount the balloon between centers on your lathe, using the ¹⁄₁₆" holes in the ends of the lamination to center the headstock and tailstock spindles. Turn the balloon to shape, using the template as a guide. (We used a ⅜" gouge and a ½" round-nosed scraper. See the photo on *top of page 48*).

3. Sand the balloon. Using a parting tool, part the bottom (basket end) of the balloon from the lathe. Use a handsaw to trim the tenon from the balloon top. Contour-sand the balloon top.

continued

⅜" nut
⅜" washer
⅜" hole
¾ × 4" dia. particleboard
Waxed paper
Temporary rubber band clamp
Waxed paper
⅜" hole
¾ × 4" dia. particleboard

CLAMPING TOGETHER ONE LAYER

⅜" washer
⅜" all-thread rod 10" long
⅜" nut

FULL-SIZED TEMPLATE

¹⁄₁₆" hole
R = 2¹⁄₁₆"
Top (maple)
¾"
¾"

¾"
Maple
Walnut

¹⁄₁₆" hole
R = 2¹⁄₁₆"
Bottom (maple)
¾"
¾"

BALLOON LAMINATION

30°

BLOCK DETAIL FULL-SIZED

3⅞" dia.
2½" dia.
2¾" dia.
1¼" dia.

Note: Top and bottom layers are solid maple

47

HIGH-FLYING BALLOON MOBILE
continued

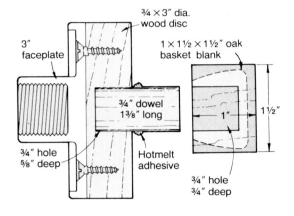

¾ × 3″ dia. wood disc

3″ faceplate

1 × 1½ × 1½″ oak basket blank

¾″ dowel 1⅜″ long

¾″ hole ⅝″ deep

Hotmelt adhesive

1″

1½″

¾″ hole ¾″ deep

With the balloom lamination mounted between centers, turn balloon to shape.

4. Cut a 3" hole in a 1"-thick piece of scrap stock. Place a piece of cloth over the hole, and place the balloon over the hole, as shown in the drawing *opposite, top left*. Position the balloon and support under your drill press, and bore a ¾" hole, centered on the ¹⁄₁₆" hole through the bottom of the balloon. Switch bits, and drill four ¹⁄₁₆" holes ½" deep into the edge of the balloon where shown on the Basket and Balloon drawing *opposite*.

Now use the template to turn the basket

1. From 1½"-thick oak (we laminated two ¾" pieces), cut a piece 1½" square. Draw diagonals on one face to find center. Hold it in a handscrew clamp, and use your drill press to bore a ¾" hole ¾" deep at the marked centerpoint.

2. Form an auxiliary faceplate like that shown *above right*. Adhere the basket blank to the ¾" dowel with a couple of drops of hotmelt adhesive. Turn the basket to shape, and sand smooth. Twist off the basket from the dowel, and remove the hotmelt.

3. Hold the basket in a handscrew clamp, and use your drill press to drill four ¹⁄₁₆" holes ½" deep in the top edge of the basket.

Add the finish, and string 'em up

1. Apply the finish to the pieces.

2. Using the Basket and Balloon drawing as a guide, hang the baskets from the balloons. Referring to the drawing titled Stringing the Balloons (*opposite*) for reference, hang the balloons from two pieces of ¼" dowel.

Project Tool List
Tablesaw
Bandsaw
Lathe
  Drive center
  Tail center
  3" Faceplate
  ⅜" Gouge
  ½" Round-nose scraper
  Parting tool
Drill press
  Bits: ¹⁄₁₆", ⅜", ¾"
Circle cutter

Note: We built the project using the tools listed. You may be able to substitute other tools or equipment for listed items you don't have. Additional common hand tools and clamps may be required to complete the project.

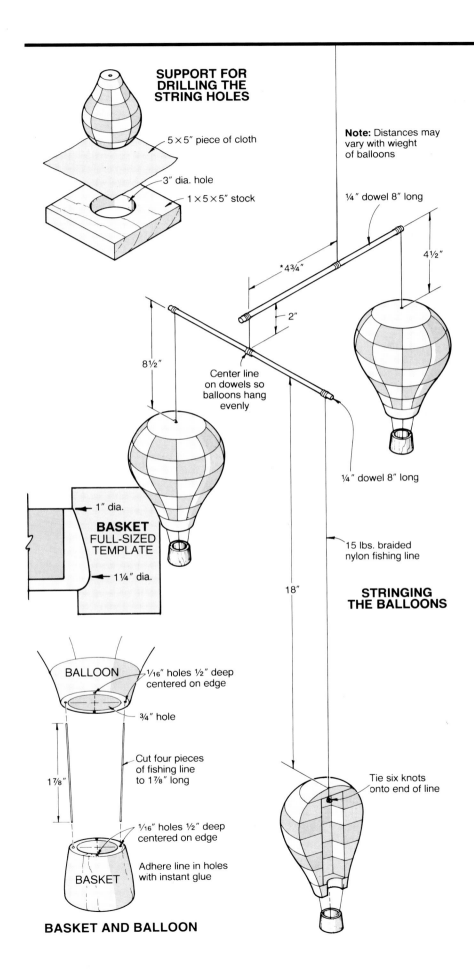

SUPPORT FOR DRILLING THE STRING HOLES

5 × 5" piece of cloth

3" dia. hole

1 × 5 × 5" stock

Note: Distances may vary with wieght of balloons

¼" dowel 8" long

* 4¾"

4½"

2"

8½"

Center line on dowels so balloons hang evenly

¼" dowel 8" long

15 lbs. braided nylon fishing line

STRINGING THE BALLOONS

18"

1" dia.

BASKET
FULL-SIZED TEMPLATE

1¼" dia.

BALLOON

1/16" holes ½" deep centered on edge

¾" hole

Cut four pieces of fishing line to 1⅞" long

1⅞"

1/16" holes ½" deep centered on edge

Adhere line in holes with instant glue

BASKET

Tie six knots onto end of line

BASKET AND BALLOON

49

DINOSAUR MIRROR

Reflect a youngster's interest in the age of dinosaurs with this brontosaurus-topped mirror. We've had a lot of fun with this mirror frame, and so will some youngster when it's hung on his or her wall.

1. Glue and edge-join enough 1¹⁄₁₆" oak stock together to form one piece measuring 10x16" long and one 8¼x16" long.

2. Joint *one* edge of each glue-up and tape the *joined* edges together where shown on the drawing *below right.*

3. Locate the radii center point on the joined edges where shown on the drawing. With compass, mark a 7½" radius and a 4¾" radius.

4. Using a square, draw a centerline through the center point and to the top of the lamination where shown.

5. Using carbon paper, transfer the dinosaur outline and eye locations to the top of the lamination from the full-sized pattern *opposite.* Position the alignment mark on the dinosaur with the marked centerline on the top oak piece.

6. Remove the tape and separate the two pieces. Band-saw the inside radius to shape on both pieces. Glue and clamp the halves together aligning the inside edges.

7. Cut the dinosaur to shape from the top piece. (We used a ⅛" blade with 14 teeth per inch on our band saw to make the cut.) Now, cut the outside frame diameter to shape. Drill a pair of ⅛" holes ⅛" deep where marked for the dinosaur's eyes.

8. Sand the inside and outside edges smooth. Rout a ⅜" rabbet ¼" deep on the *back* side of the frame for the mirror. Rout a ¼" round-over on the *front-outside* edge, being careful not to rout into the dinosaur's head or tail openings. Rout a ¼" round-over on the *front-inside* and *back-outside* edges.

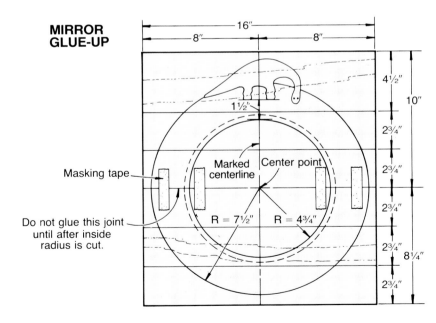

MIRROR GLUE-UP

Masking tape

Do not glue this joint until after inside radius is cut.

Marked centerline

Center point

R = 7½"

R = 4¾"

16"

8"

8"

4½"

10"

1½"

2¾"

2¾"

2¾"

2¾"

2¾"

8¼"

9. Finish-sand the mirror frame and dinosaur. Stain and finish as desired. (We used latex acrylic paint on the dinosaur and a light stain and Minwax Antique Oil on the frame. Spray paint would also work on the dinosaur.)

10. Have the mirror cut to shape (we had ours cut ⅛" undersize to allow for expansion of the wood).

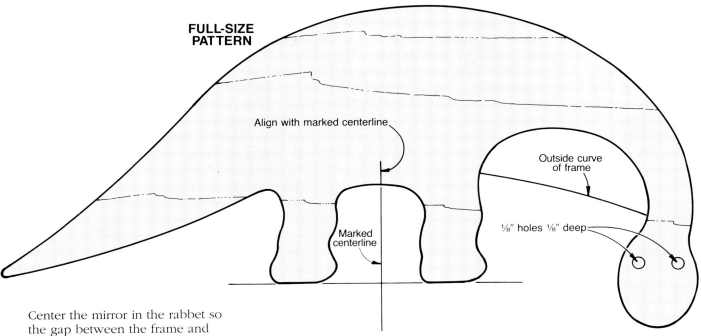

FULL-SIZE PATTERN

Align with marked centerline

Marked centerline

Outside curve of frame

⅛" holes ⅛" deep

Center the mirror in the rabbet so the gap between the frame and mirror is equal all the way around. Adhere the mirror to the frame by running a bead of silicone sealant in the gap around the mirror where shown in the Rabbet detail.

11. Fasten a sawtoothed hanger to the back of the mirror frame, hang on a wall, and slide the dinosaur in place. Finally, stand back, look in the mirror, and ask "who's the fairest woodworker of them all?"

Supplies

Carbon paper, ⅛×10⅛" mirror, sawtoothed hanger with 2—#6×¾" roundhead wood screws, silicone sealant, stain, finish, paint for dinosaur.

Project Tool List

Tablesaw
Jointer
Bandsaw
Router
 Bits: ⅜" rabbet, ¼" round-over
Drill press
 ⅛" bit
Finishing sander

Note: *We built the project using the tools listed. You may be able to substitute other tools or equipment for listed items you don't have. Additional common hand tools and clamps may be required to complete the project.*

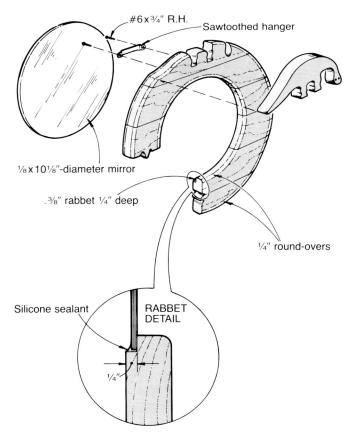

#6 x ¾" R.H.

Sawtoothed hanger

⅛ x 10⅛"-diameter mirror

⅜" rabbet ¼" deep

¼" round-overs

Silicone sealant

RABBET DETAIL

¼"

LAMP-NESS CREATURE

There's a mystery surrounding our Lamp-Ness creature—that is, until you press down on the creature's tail. This action lights the lamp, amusing little onlookers who may be standing nearby. With its 11-inch, clip-on shade and 40-watt bulb, the lamp stands 16 inches tall, making it perfect for a child's dresser.

First, form the base and the water layer

1. Rip and crosscut two pieces of ¾" pine and 1 piece of ¼" hardboard to 9" square. Draw diagonals to find and mark the centerpoints on the three squares.

2. To enlarge the grid patterns of the base layers A and B *(opposite)*, draw a 1" grid on two sheets of 8½x11", or larger, writing paper. Select a grid intersection that's close to the center on each sheet and make it the centerpoint for that pattern. Next, lay out the shapes of the two base layer patterns, using the centerpoints as reference points. Using the dimensions, mark the points on your grids where the patterns intersect the pattern grid lines. Using a straightedge, draw lines to connect the points. Finally, use a compass or draw the curved lines freehand to complete the patterns.

3. Trace the full-sized pattern of layer A onto one pine square, and the pattern of B onto the other pine square. (We backed the patterns with carbon paper. To center the patterns we pushed a tack through the centerpoints on the patterns and into the centerpoint of each square.) Remove the paper patterns. Draw a 4" radius circle on the top of the square with the pattern of layer A.

4. Rip and crosscut a piece of ¼" hardboard to 9x13". Using the same techniques as explained in steps 2 and 3, enlarge, and then trace the pattern of the water layer C *(opposite)* onto the hardboard. Include the locations of the screws, the body parts, and the rectangular tail cutout from the pattern.

5. Drill all of the ⅜" holes in the two squares and the piece where indicated. Next, change bits and drill the four ⁵⁄₆₄" screw holes through the water layer. Finally, countersink the holes on the underside.

6. Next, chuck a ⅛" straight or veining bit in your router's collet. Rout the ⅛" groove ⅛" deep in the *top* surface of layer A. (We used a straightedge to guide the router as shown *opposite, top left.)*

7. Next, switch to a ¼" straight router bit. Turn the square for layer B upside down, and mark the position for the lamp cord groove. (See the gridded pattern for location.) Place the bit in the ⅜" centerhole. Now, clamp a straightedge in place to guide the router, and rout the ¼"-deep groove.

8. Stack square A on top of square B. Insert a ⅜" dowel through the two centerholes to align the squares. Using double-faced tape, stick the ¼"-thick hardboard square for the base layer (D) to the bottom of the stack. Now, using a band-saw, saw the assembled pieces to shape, cutting just outside the circular line. Separate the parts.

9. Using a scrollsaw, cut out the switch cavity area in layer A as shown *below bottom*. Next, cut out the switch cavity in layer B, and the tail opening in water layer C.

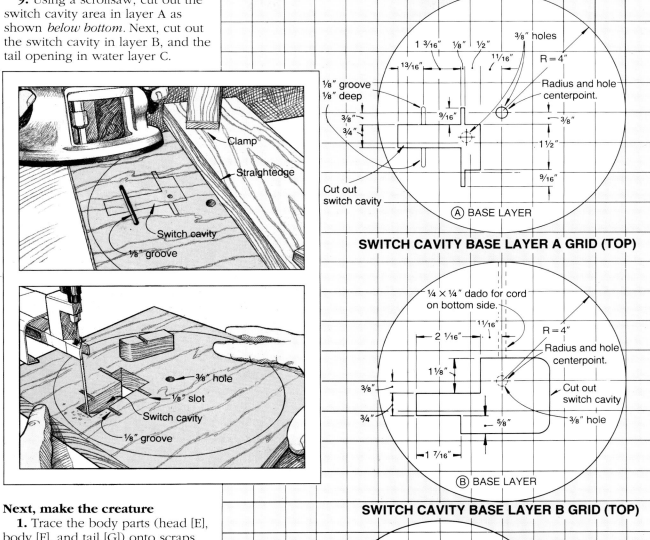

Clamp

Straightedge

Switch cavity

⅛" groove

⅜" hole

⅛" slot

Switch cavity

⅛" groove

Next, make the creature

1. Trace the body parts (head [E], body [F], and tail [G]) onto scraps of ¾" maple, using the full-sized patterns shown on *page 54*. Mark the eye hole on the head, and the hole location for the pivot-pin on the tail.

2. Back the tail piece with scrap, and drill the ³⁄₃₂" hole. Next, saw all body parts to shape. (We cut just outside the line, and then sanded to the line.) Sand to break the hard edges. *Do not* sand along the bottoms edges. Finally, drill the ³⁄₁₆" eye hole through the head.

Now, assemble the lamp

1. Apply woodworker's glue to the top surface of layer B. Next,
continued

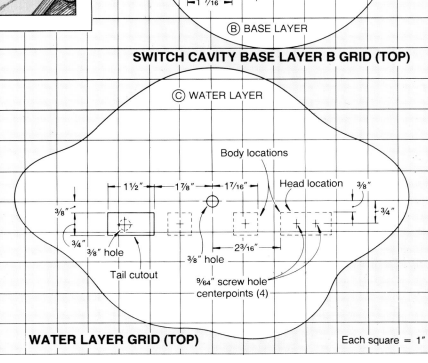

⅜" holes

1 ³⁄₁₆"   ⅛"   ½"

13⁄₁₆"   11⁄₁₆"   R = 4"

⅛" groove ⅛" deep

Radius and hole centerpoint.

⅜"   9⁄₁₆"   ⅜"

¾"   1½"

Cut out switch cavity   9⁄₁₆"

Ⓐ BASE LAYER

SWITCH CAVITY BASE LAYER A GRID (TOP)

¼ × ¼" dado for cord on bottom side.

2 1⁄₁₆"   11⁄₁₆"   R = 4"

1⅛"

Radius and hole centerpoint.

⅜"   Cut out switch cavity

¾"   5⁄₈"   ⅜" hole

1 7⁄₁₆"

Ⓑ BASE LAYER

SWITCH CAVITY BASE LAYER B GRID (TOP)

Ⓒ WATER LAYER

Body locations

1½"   1⅞"   17⁄₁₆"   Head location   ⅜"

⅜"   ¾"

⅜"   2³⁄₁₆"

¾"   ⅜" hole

Tail cutout   ⅜" hole

9⁄₆₄" screw hole centerpoints (4)

WATER LAYER GRID (TOP)   Each square = 1"

LAMP-NESS CREATURE
continued

place layer A on top of it, top side up, as shown on the Base Assembly drawing at *right*. Orient the layers so the switch cavities in both align where shown. Clamp until the glue dries.

2. Drill and countersink four equally spaced screw holes around the periphery in layer D, ½" in from the edge. Remove the clamps from the base after the glue has dried, and temporarily screw part D to the *bottom* of B. Using a stationary disc sander, sand the assembly round. Remove layer D from the base.

Note: *You can purchase the electrical lamp parts needed for the project, excluding the shade, as a kit from our Buying Guide source* opposite.

3. To make the switch support (H), rip and crosscut a piece of maple to the dimensions in the Bill of Materials. Next, drill the ⅜" hole using dimensions on the Base Assembly drawing. Mount the switch. Now, insert the switch support in the slots in layer A.

4. Cut the head off an 8d finish nail so you end up with a 1¾"-long pin. Insert it through the hole in the tail. Now, place the tail into the

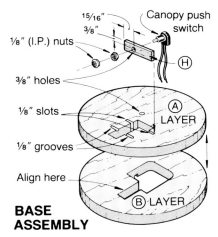

BASE ASSEMBLY

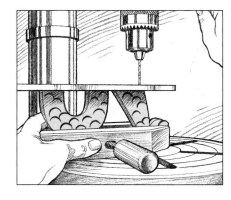

base so the nail lies in the ⅛" grooves. (See the Exploded View drawing *opposite*.)

5. Place the water layer over the base so the tail protrudes through the rectangular cutout and the ⅜" hole aligns with the hole in the base assembly. Test to make sure the tail operates the switch. If necessary, sand the tail or the tail opening so it crisply clicks the switch on and off.

6. Remove the water layer from the base. Paint all parts. (We painted the base assembly flat

black, the water light blue, and the creature orange with scales outlined in black.)

7. With double-faced tape, stick the creature's head and body to the top of the water layer where indicated on the pattern. Next, turn the assembly upside down and clamp the creature in a wood screw clamp as shown *above*. Now, using the predrilled holes as guides, drill the ³⁄₃₂" pilot holes ½" deep into the body parts. Drive the screws. Remove the clamp from the creature, and place the water layer back on the base.

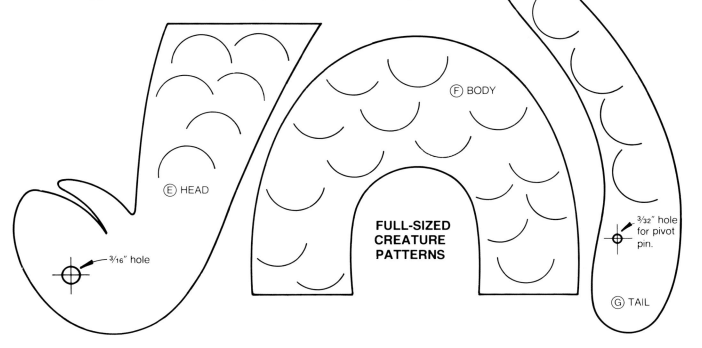

E HEAD

³⁄₁₆" hole

F BODY

FULL-SIZED CREATURE PATTERNS

³⁄₃₂" hole for pivot pin.

G TAIL

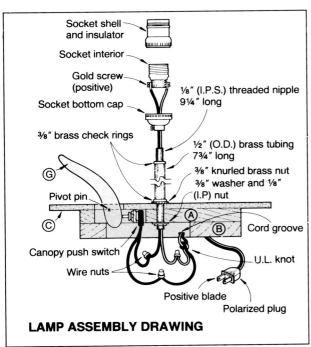

LAMP ASSEMBLY DRAWING

Socket shell and insulator
Socket interior
Gold screw (positive)
Socket bottom cap
⅜" brass check rings
⅛" (I.P.S.) threaded nipple 9¼" long
½" (O.D.) brass tubing 7¾" long
⅜" knurled brass nut
⅜" washer and ⅛" (I.P) nut
G
Pivot pin
C
Canopy push switch
Wire nuts
A
B
Cord groove
U.L. knot
Positive blade
Polarized plug

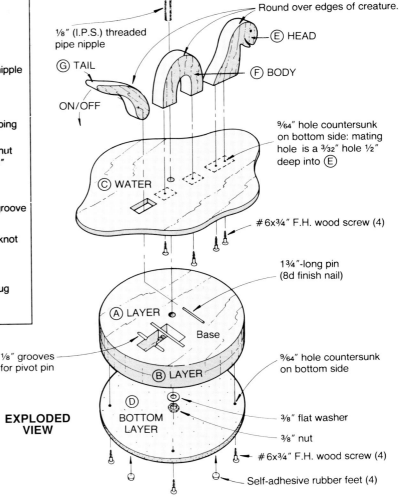

EXPLODED VIEW

⅛" (I.P.S.) threaded pipe nipple
G TAIL
ON/OFF
Round over edges of creature.
E HEAD
F BODY
C WATER
9/64" hole countersunk on bottom side: mating hole is a 3/32" hole ½" deep into E
#6x¾" F.H. wood screw (4)
1¾"-long pin (8d finish nail)
A LAYER
Base
⅛" grooves for pivot pin
B LAYER
9/64" hole countersunk on bottom side
D BOTTOM LAYER
⅜" flat washer
⅜" nut
#6x¾" F.H. wood screw (4)
Self-adhesive rubber feet (4)

Bill of Materials

Part	Initial Size*			Mat.	Qty.
	T	W	L		
A*	¾"	9"	9"	P	1
B*	¾"	9"	9"	P	1
C*	¼"	9"	13"	HB	1
D*	¼"	9"	9"	HB	1
E*	¾"	3½"	3½"	M	1
F*	¾"	3"	3½"	M	1
G*	¾"	1½"	5"	M	1
H	⅛"	¾"	2½"	M	1

Parts marked with an * are cut large initially, and then cut to final size. Please read instructions before cutting.

Material Key: P—pine, HB—hardboard, M—maple
Supplies: 8—#6X¾" F.H. wood screws, 4—self-adhesive rubber feet, 8d finish nail, double-faced tape, glue, carbon paper, writing paper, paint.

8. Install the threaded rod through the ⅜" holes in the water layer and the base. Add the washer and the steel nut to the rod's bottom end. Now, assemble the rest of the lamp parts as shown on the Lamp Assembly drawing, *above.*

9. Wire the lamp as shown on the Lamp Assembly drawing. To prevent marring of the dresser top, apply self-adhesive feet (available at hardware stores) to the bottom of the base. Now top the lamp with the shade of your choice. (We suggest using a 10" or 12" Empire clip-on lamp shade.)

Buying Guide

• **Lamp kit.** Threaded rod, polished-brass tubing, brass socket, brass knurled nut, steel nut, brass check rings, steel washer, 8' electrical cord, and canopy push switch. For current prices, contact The Lamp Shop, 3215 Forest Ave., Des Moines IA 50311.

Project Tool List

Tablesaw
Bandsaw
Scrollsaw
Disc sander
Drill press
   Bits: 3/32", 9/64", 3/16", ⅜"
Router
   Bits: ⅛" straight or veining, ¼" straight
Finishing sander

SAFARI SHELVES

Stop the hunting... for toys! It makes more sense to round up all the pieces and put them in plastic storage boxes—until the sun rises on yet another adventure in imagination.

Cut the cabinet parts first

1. Using the dimensions listed on the Bill of Materials, rip and crosscut two ends (A), one back (B), and three shelves (C) from ¾"-thick plywood. (We used birch.) See the Cutting Diagram *opposite* for how we laid out the parts on our stock.

Note: We sized each shelf to conveniently hold one large 5⅞X14X28" under-the-bed storage box, or three shoe-box-sized 4½X7½X13" plastic storage containers. Box sizes vary among manufacturers, so we suggest you buy the boxes first, and if necessary, adjust your cabin-et dimensions to accommodate them.

2. With a compass, scribe a 1½" radius on the corners of both end panels. Cut these corners with a sabersaw, sawing just outside the line. Next, sand each corner to the line. (We used our disc sander as shown *opposite, lower left.)* Sand carefully to keep the edge square for ease in installing the plywood veneer edging tape.

3. To finish the end-panel edges, measure the perimeter of one panel, and then cut two strips of ¹³⁄₁₆"-wide plywood veneer edging to that length plus 1". (We bought birch veneer edging at a home-center.) Brush two light coats of contact adhesive evenly on the inside face of each veneer strip and along the edges of both end panels. If you aren't familiar with contact adhesives, follow the directions on the product label, and test on scrap first. When the adhesive reaches the right tack (according to label directions), start at the bottom and apply the edging to the end panels

as shown *opposite, lower right.* Trim off the excess with scissors or knife.

4. Adhere a strip of veneer plywood edging to the top edge of the back panel, using the same technique. Now, carefully sand the panel edges with 220-grit sandpaper.

5. From ¾"-thick solid stock (we used birch), rip and crosscut three 1½X25¼" shelf aprons (D). Glue and nail one apron to the front edge of each shelf, aligning the aprons along the top edge and at the ends. (For this, we used yellow

woodworker's glue and 6d finish nails.) Now, finish-sand all parts.

6. From the same hardwood stock rip and crosscut six ¾X¾X12¼" support cleats (E). Next, drill ⁵⁄₃₂" shank holes in each cleat so you can attach them to the side panels and to the shelves. Now, screw a pair of cleats to the underside of each shelf, aligning each with the shelf end.

7. From scrap, cut a 1"-wide 24"-long spacer, a 2¼"-wide 15"-long spacer, and two 8¼"-square spacers. You'll use them to space the shelves when assembling the cabinet.

Let's assemble the cabinet

1. Lay an end panel on its side. Align the 1"-wide spacer along the back edge and clamp it in place. Clamp the 2¼"-wide spacer along the bottom of the panel. Now, position the bottom shelf against the spacers and screw the bottom shelf cleat to the end as shown on the Exploded View drawing on *page 58*. (We used #8X1¼" flathead wood screws.)

2. Stand the remaining two shelves on the end panel with the back edge against the 1"-wide spacer. Place your two 8¼"-square spacers between the shelves as shown on *page 58, bottom*. Screw a shelf cleat to each end. Next, turn the cabinet end for end. Attach each shelf to the second end, using the same spacers and techniques to position and attach them.

3. Remove the spacers, lay the cabinet on its front, and square the case. (We used a framing square and measured diagonally from corner to corner.) Next, lay the back panel (with best face down) over the back edge of the shelves, aligning the bottom edge with the bottom of the shelf cleats. Now, locate the shelves, and then drill and countersink ⁵⁄₃₂" shank holes through the back. Drill ⁷⁄₆₄" pilot holes into the shelves. (We drilled three holes into each.) Drive a #8X1½" flathead wood screw in each hole.

Shape the giraffes next

1. To make a full-sized giraffe pattern, first tape together sheets of paper to form a 17X45" rectangle. Now, start at a corner and scribe 1" squares across the entire surface of the paper.

2. Using the gridded Giraffe pattern on *page 59* as your guide,
continued

Cutting Diagram

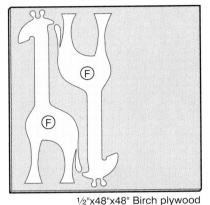

½"x48"x48" Birch plywood

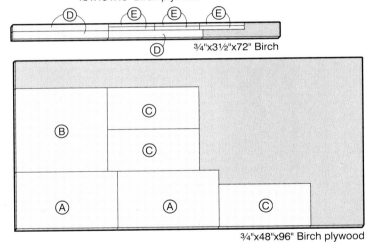

¾"x3½"x72" Birch

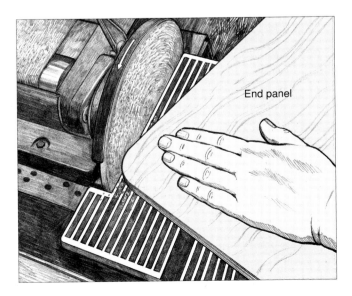

¾"x48"x96" Birch plywood

Bill of Materials				
Part	**Finished Size**			**Mat.**	**Qty.**

Part	T	W	L	Mat.	Qty.
A end	¾"	15"	28"	P	2
B back	¾"	25¼"	24⅛"	P	1
C shelf	¾"	12¼"	25¼"	P	3
D apron	¾"	1½"	25¼"	B	3
E cleat	¾"	¾"	12¼"	B	6
F giraffe	½"	15½"	44½"	P	2

Material Key: B—birch; P—birch plywood
Supplies: #8X1¼" and 1½" flathead wood screws, four—⅞" tack glides, ¹³⁄₁₆" X 8' plywood edging, 6d finish nails, contact adhesive, paint, finish, plastic storage boxes.

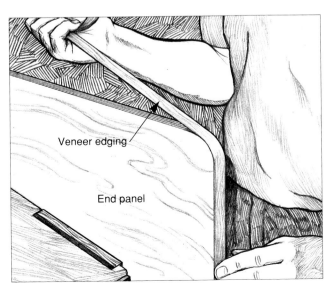

End panel

Veneer edging

End panel

SAFARI SHELVES
continued

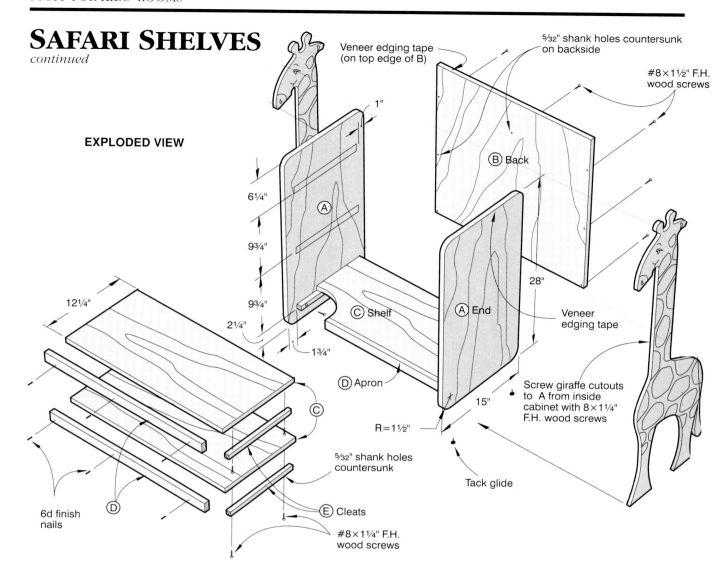

EXPLODED VIEW

Veneer edging tape
(on top edge of B)

5/32" shank holes countersunk
on backside

#8×1½" F.H.
wood screws

B Back

1"

6¼"

9¾"

A

9¾"

28"

2¼"

12¼"

1¾"

C Shelf

A End

Veneer
edging tape

D Apron

Screw giraffe cutouts
to A from inside
cabinet with 8×1¼"
F.H. wood screws

15"

R=1½"

5/32" shank holes
countersunk

Tack glide

6d finish
nails

D

C

E Cleats

#8×1¼" F.H.
wood screws

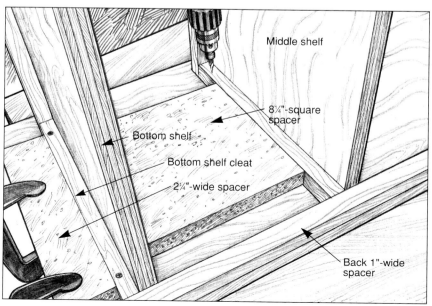

Middle shelf

8¼"-square
spacer

Bottom shelf

Bottom shelf cleat

2¼"-wide spacer

Back 1"-wide
spacer

draw the giraffe outline, eyes, nose, mouth, and spots onto your gridded paper. (When working with gridded patterns, we first plot the points where the pattern lines cross the grid lines. Then, we draw the lines connecting the points. We use French curves to help draw the curving pattern lines.)

3. With scissors, cut around the pattern, leaving about a 1" margin. Using transfer or carbon paper, trace one outline and all body details onto your ½"-thick birch plywood. Turn the pattern over and trace a second giraffe. Now, using a sabersaw, saw both giraffes (F) to shape. Sand the cut edges on both giraffe cutouts.

4. Position your pattern on the opposite side of each cutout. Next, transfer the body spots, the eyes, and all other facial features to the portion of each giraffe that extends above the cabinet.

Now, finish the cabinet and paint your giraffes

1. Erase unwanted marks on the giraffes. Next, seal the wood surface (we applied a light coat of sanding sealer), let it dry, and then paint the black-and-white eyes, the brown body spots, and brown facial lines. (We used acrylic paints available at crafts stores.) After the paints dry, seal the surfaces with clear polyurethane or lacquer.

2. Apply the finish of your choice to the cabinet. (We left the birch unstained. Then we applied one coat of sanding sealer and two coats of clear polyurethane, sanding after each application dried with 320-grit sandpaper.)

3. Drive tack glides into the bottom edge of each end panel, centering them 3" in from each corner. If you wish to make the cabinet more maneuverable, simply attach casters to the bottom of the

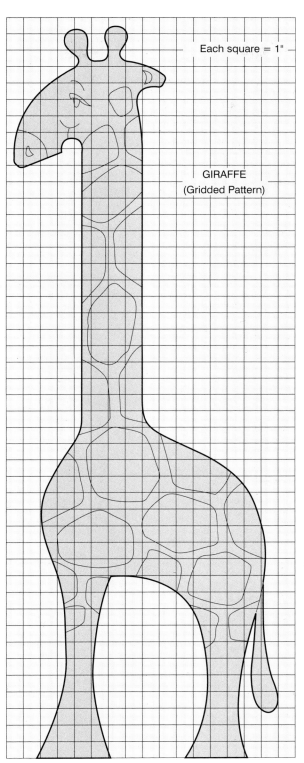

Each square = 1"

GIRAFFE
(Gridded Pattern)

panels instead. Next, attach the giraffes to the ends. (We clamped them in place, and then drilled screw holes from the inside of the cabinet. After countersinking each of these holes, we drove #8X1¼" flathead wood screws through the end panels and into the giraffes to secure them.)

4. Outfit the cabinet with the plastic storage boxes of your choice. You can buy reasonably priced clear or nearly clear plastic storage boxes similar to those we used on our shelves at stores that sell kitchen and household supplies.

Project Tool List
Tablesaw
Portable jigsaw
Disc sander
Drill press
Portable drill
  Bits: ⁷⁄₆₄", ⁵⁄₃₂"
Finishing sander

Note: *We built the project using the tools listed. You may be able to substitute other tools or equipment for listed items you don't have. Additional common hand tools and clamps may be required to complete the project.*

A YOUNG SKIPPER'S STOOL

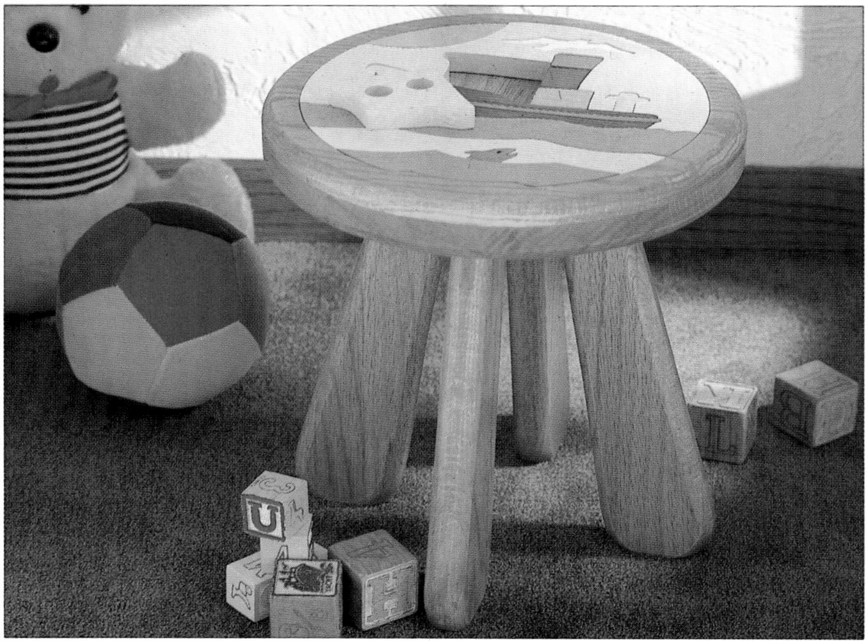

Ahoy mates! Get your sea legs beneath you and navigate through a puzzle project for your favorite little sailor.

Steady as she goes. Begin with the legs and braces

1. Prepare a leg pattern by first drawing 1" squares across a sheet of paper measuring at least 5" wide and 12" long. Next, referring to the Gridded Leg pattern on *page 62,* draw the leg outline on your gridded sheet. (When working with patterns like these, we first plot the points where the pattern lines cross the grid lines. Then, we draw the lines connecting these points.)

2. From 1 1/16"-thick stock (we used red oak stair tread), rip and crosscut four leg blanks (A) to 5X12". See the Cutting Diagram at *right* for how we laid out our stock. Next, rip and crosscut two crossbraces (B) to the dimensions listed in the Bill of Materials.

3. With your tablesaw, cut a dado centered in the top edge of each leg blank as dimensioned on the Leg Assembly drawing *opposite.* (We elevated the saw blade 2" above the tabletop, and set the fence 3/8" from the blade. Next, we stood the leg blank on end, and using a pushstick for safety, cut a kerf. We then rotated the piece and cut the second kerf. After sawing the kerfs in each leg blank, we moved the fence in 1/8" increments and sawed away the material between the two kerfs.)

4. Cut tenons on both ends of each crossbrace following the Leg Assembly drawing dimensions. (To cut the tenons, we used the dado in one of the legs as a guide to set the fence the required distance [3/8"] from the blade.) To make the cuts, stand the crossbraces on end and against the fence, then as shown *opposite,* cut the first kerf. (We tested our setting on scrap first.) Rotate the piece to cut the opposite kerf. After you've kerfed both sides on each end of both braces, lower the saw blade to match the kerf depth (3/8"). Now, cut away the waste to expose the tenons.

5. Position and trace the leg pattern onto a leg blank. Scrollsaw this leg to shape and sand the cut edges. (We used a #9 blade with 11 teeth per inch.) Use this leg as your pattern and trace its outline onto the three remaining leg blanks. Saw all legs to shape and sand the edges.

6. Locate the center of each crossbrace. Lay out the 1 1/16"-wide, 1" deep notch shown on the Exploded View drawing. Saw the notches.

Bill of Materials

Part	Finished Size T	W	L	Mat.	Qty.
A leg	1 1/16"	4 7/16"	11 1/8"	O	4
B brace	1 1/16"	2"	9"	O	2
C* seat	1 1/16"	12" diam.		O	1
D* puzzle	1/2"	12" diam.		O	1

*Laminated from narrower pieces and sawed to shape. Read the instructions carefully before cutting.

Material Key: O—oak
Supplies: 3/8" dowel stock, #8X2 1/2" flathead wood screws, paints, finish.

CUTTING DIAGRAM

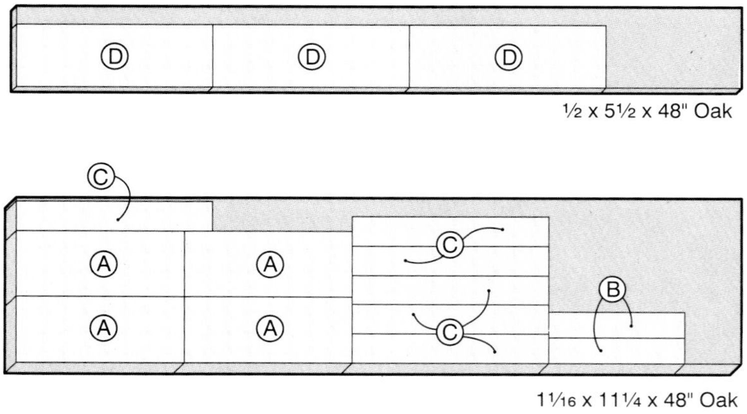
D
D
D
1/2 x 5 1/2 x 48" Oak
C
A
A
C
A
A
B
C
1 1/16 x 11 1/4 x 48" Oak

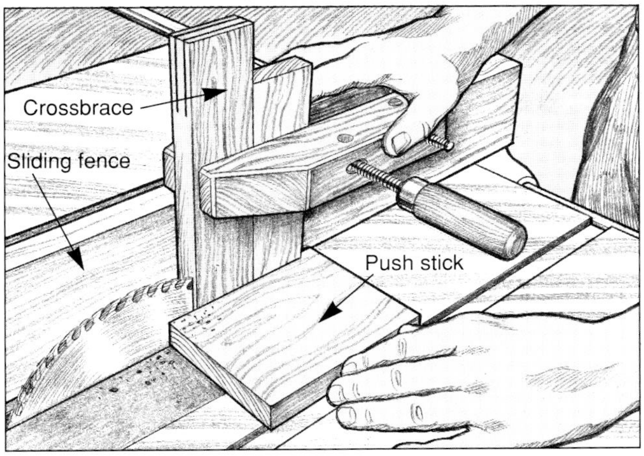
Crossbrace
Sliding fence
Push stick

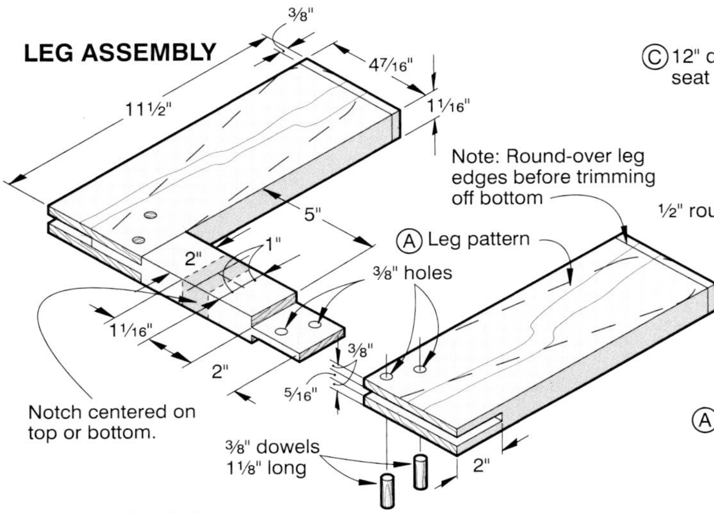
LEG ASSEMBLY
3/8"
4 7/16"
1 1/16"
11 1/2"
Note: Round-over leg edges before trimming off bottom
5"
1"
2"
Ⓐ Leg pattern
3/8" holes
1 1/16"
2"
3/8"
5/16"
Notch centered on top or bottom.
3/8" dowels 1 1/8" long
2"

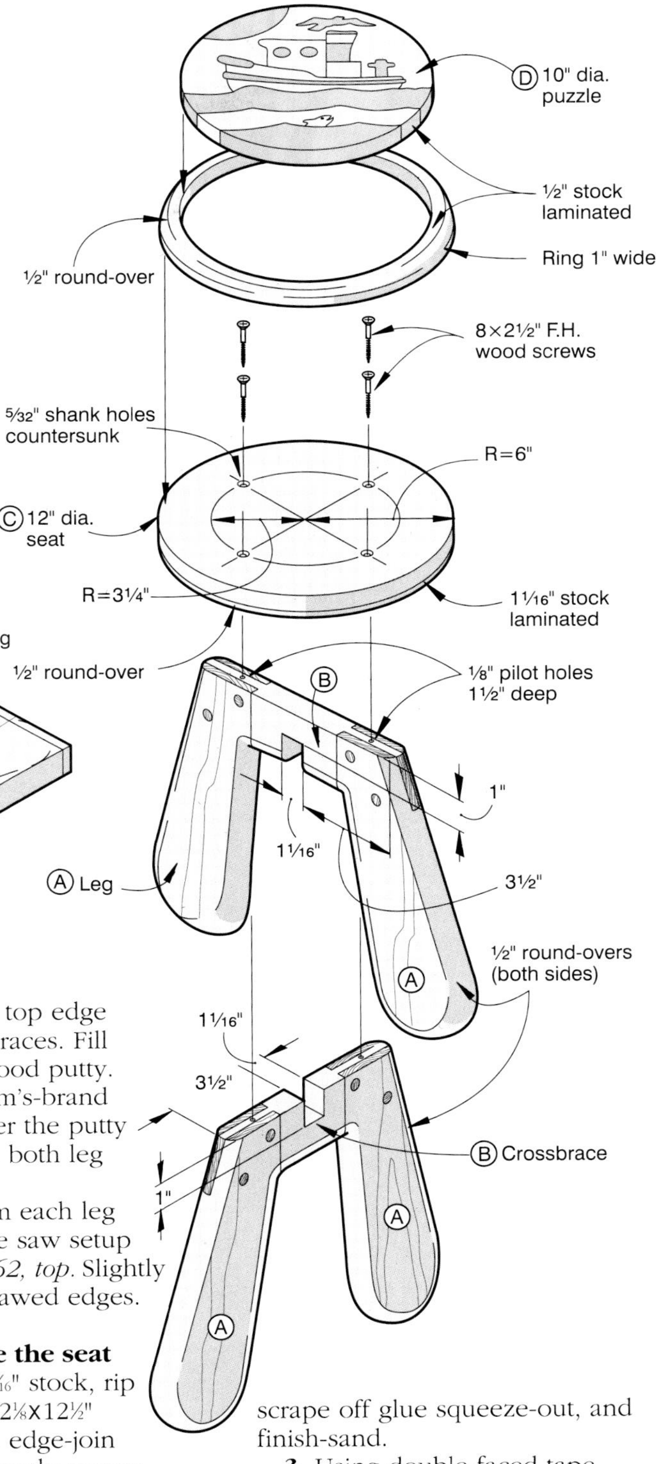
Ⓓ 10" dia. puzzle
1/2" stock laminated
Ring 1" wide
1/2" round-over
8×2 1/2" F.H. wood screws
5/32" shank holes countersunk
R=6"
Ⓒ 12" dia. seat
R=3 1/4"
1 1/16" stock laminated
1/2" round-over
Ⓑ
1/8" pilot holes 1 1/2" deep
1"
1 1/16"
Ⓐ Leg
3 1/2"
1/2" round-overs (both sides)
Ⓐ
1 1/16"
3 1/2"
Ⓑ Crossbrace
1"
Ⓐ
Ⓐ

Assemble both legs

1. From 3/8" dowel, crosscut eight 1 1/8"-long lengths. Next, dry-assemble the legs and crossbraces, making sure one notch faces up, the other faces down. Square all parts and locate the hole center-points for the dowels where dimensioned on the Leg pattern. Drill these 3/8" holes through the leg assemblies. (To ensure perfect hole alignment and the strongest possible joints, we drilled the first hole and inserted a dowel partway through it before drilling the second hole.)

2. Glue and assemble each leg pair (A) and the crossbraces (B) as shown *above*. Glue a dowel in each hole. After the glue dries, trim off all dowels and the tenons extending beyond the legs. Sand all cut edges on the assembled legs.

3. Using a 1/2" round-over router bit with a 3/8" bearing, round over all edges on the two leg assemblies except along the top edge of the legs and braces. Fill any gaps with wood putty. (We used Durham's-brand water putty.) After the putty dries, finish-sand both leg assemblies.

4. Trim 3/8" from each leg bottom, using the saw setup shown on *page 62, top*. Slightly round over the sawed edges.

Next, let's make the seat

1. From the 1 1/16" stock, rip and crosscut six 2 1/8x12 1/2" pieces. Glue and edge-join them to form a nearly square lamination. Clamp and let it set overnight.

2. From 1/2"-thick stock, rip and crosscut three 4 1/8x12 1/2" pieces for the puzzle layer (D). Glue-join these pieces into a square and clamp. After the glue cures, remove the clamps from both laminations, scrape off glue squeeze-out, and finish-sand.

3. Using double-faced tape, adhere the 1/2"-thick lamination to the top of the 1 1/16"-thick lamination, and align edges. (We ran the grain of both pieces the same direction.) Trim the laminations to identical size. Draw diagonals on both pieces to mark centerpoints. On

continued

A YOUNG SKIPPER'S STOOL
continued

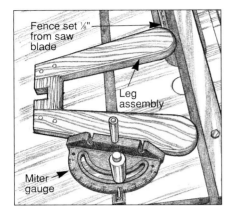

Fence set ⅛" from saw blade

Leg assembly

Miter gauge

the bottom of the 1¼₆"-thick lamination, scribe a 3¼"-radius (6½"-diameter) circle and one 6"-radius (12"-diameter) circle. Scribe a 5"-radius (10"-diameter) circle on the ½"-thick lamination.

4. Copy the full-sized Puzzle pattern *opposite* and cut it to shape. (We photocopied our work copy.) Now, center and adhere your pattern inside the 10" circle on the face of the ½"-thick lamination. (We used spray adhesive.)

5. Bandsaw both laminations round, sawing just outside the 12"-diameter line. Sand the sawed edge on both laminations. Now, separate the laminations and remove the tape.

6. Drill a ¼₆" start hole through the 10"-diameter line on the ½"-thick puzzle layer. Next, scrollsaw along the line to separate the 10"-diameter disc from the ring. Bore the two ⅝" cabin holes. Drill a ¼₆" hole for the fish eye, and for a start hole at the bird's wing tip. Now, scrollsaw the puzzle. (We used a #5 blade.) Remove the pattern from the puzzle pieces. Sand the puzzle edges for clearance.

7. Center and glue the puzzle ring to the 1¼₆"-thick lamination as shown on the Exploded View drawing. Clamp. After the glue dries, remove the clamps and sand the edge flush. Fill any voids with wood putty. Now, round over the edges on the seat and ring with a ½" round-over router bit. Drill and countersink the ⁵⁄₃₂" holes in the seat where shown.

Now you're really sailing

1. Assemble the legs by interlocking the notched braces. Center the seat on top of the legs and align the holes with the braces. Drill ⅛" pilot holes (through the existing seat holes) 1½" deep into the braces. Drive a #8x2½" flathead wood screw in each hole. Fill the holes with putty.

2. To paint the puzzle parts, you may follow our color scheme or create your own. (We brushed on child-safe enamel paints.) Apply the finish of your choice to the stool. (We brushed one coat of sanding sealer and two coats of clear lacquer on the unpainted parts, sanding after each coat dried with 220-grit sandpaper to level the finish.) Allow all puzzle pieces to dry thoroughly.

Project Tool List
Tablesaw
Bandsaw
Scrollsaw
Portable drill
Drill press
  Bits: ¼₆", ⅛", ⁵⁄₃₂", ⅜", ⅝"
Disc sander
Router
  ½" round-over bit
Finishing sander

Note: *We built the project using the tools listed. You may be able to substitute other tools or equipment for listed items you don't have. Additional common hand tools and clamps may be required to complete the project.*

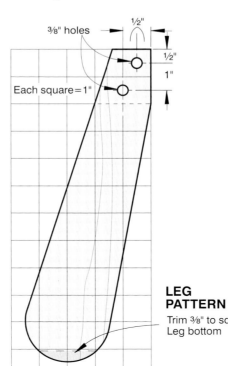

Finger holes

5

3/8" holes

1/2"

1/2"

1"

Each square = 1"

LEG PATTERN
Trim ⅜" to square
Leg bottom

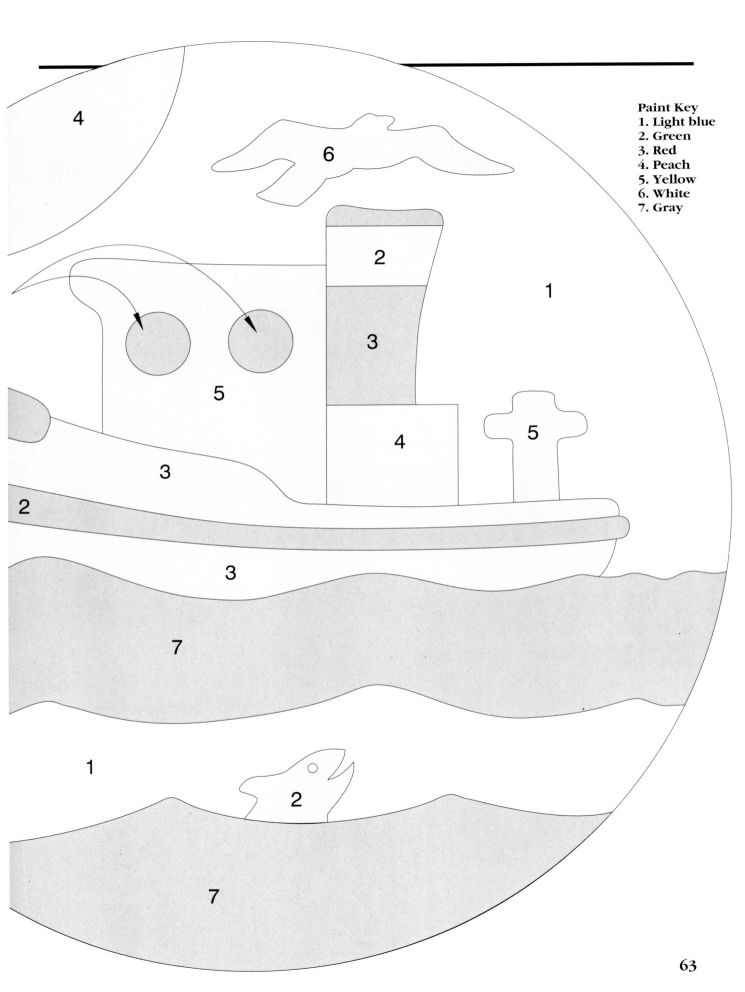

Paint Key
1. Light blue
2. Green
3. Red
4. Peach
5. Yellow
6. White
7. Gray

GIFTS, GAGS, AND GIZMOS

With these projects for toys and puzzles you'll be able to delight kids. Craft a ferris wheel, a jelly bean dispenser, an armored-car bank, a puzzle map, or another imaginative gift.

FERRIS WHEEL

Gently turn the spokes of this midway attraction, and you may soon find a child or two at your side, watching in delight as the seats rise and fall in rotation. Made from walnut and oak, our Ferris wheel stands over 14½" tall and holds up to eight wooden people. For you would-be Santas, this gift idea is a must.

First, cut the wheel spokes

1. From ¾" stock (we used oak), rip and crosscut the four spokes (A) to size using the dimensions listed in the Bill of Materials on *page 66*. (To avoid confusion, we marked the *outside* face on each spoke.) Next, mark the dados for the half-laps on the *inside* face of two spokes and on the *outside* face of the other two. Now, mark the centerpoints for the dowel holes at the ends of each spoke. Also, mark the ⅜" radii at the ends of the spokes.

2. Drill the eight ¼" dowel holes on the spoke ends. (It's critical these holes be drilled identically, so we tacked a small right-angle jig to a large piece of scrap, and then clamped it to the drill press table as shown *below*. This helped us position the spoke ends in exactly

the same place.) Sand the radii on the spoke ends. (We used a stationary disk/belt sander.) Now, set the spokes aside, we'll cut the dadoes for the half-lap joints later.

3. Next, rip and crosscut the oak wheel spacer (B) to ¾x¾x2¾". Mark the centerpoint on one end of the spacer, and chuck a ¹³⁄₃₂" bit in your drill. Clamp the spacer in a handscrew clamp as shown *below,* and then clamp the assembly to the table. Check the piece for square (we used a try square), and drill a hole halfway through the block. Turn the block end-for-end, reclamp it, and complete the drilling.

Next, make the uprights

1. Rip and crosscut the two 1×9" uprights (C) from ¾" oak stock. Mark a ½" radius on one end of both pieces. Next, mark the centerpoints for the ⅜" dowel holes on the inside face at the same ends.

2. Back the upright pieces with scrap, and drill the ⅜" holes. Now sand the radii on the ends.

Now, shape the base

1. From ¾" walnut stock, cut the base (D) to 5½x11". With a compass, mark a 2¾" radius on

both ends. Next, make a light pencil mark along both outside edges 5" in from each end.

2. Mount a dado onto your tablesaw that's set to cut a ½"-wide dado, ¾" deep. Next, set your saw's miter gauge at a right angle to the blade, and screw a wood fence to it. Now, carefully align and cut the 1"-wide notches for the uprights in the base between the marks you penciled on the sides. (As shown *below,* we made two cuts for each, first cutting to the pencil mark on the right, and then on the left.) Leave the dado on your tablesaw for now. You'll use it again.

3. Using a bandsaw or portable jigsaw, cut the rounded ends, and sand the edges. Next, chuck a ¼" round-over bit into your table-mounted router, and round-over the top edge of the base. Finish-sand the base. (We temporarily filled the notches with ¾x1" scrap pieces while routing and sanding the base.)

4. Lower the dado blade in your tablesaw to ¼" above the table. Make a test cut in scrap to ensure it measures exactly ¼" deep. Now, retrieve the spoke parts you put aside earlier and dado the half-laps.

continued

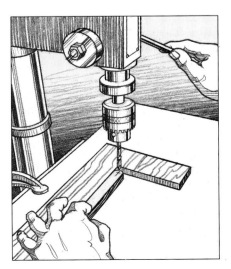
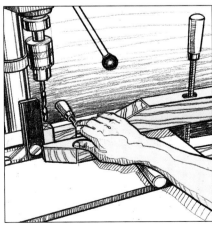
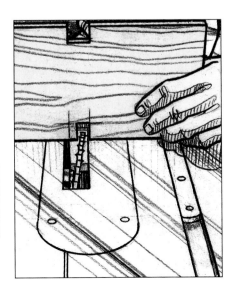

FERRIS WHEEL
continued

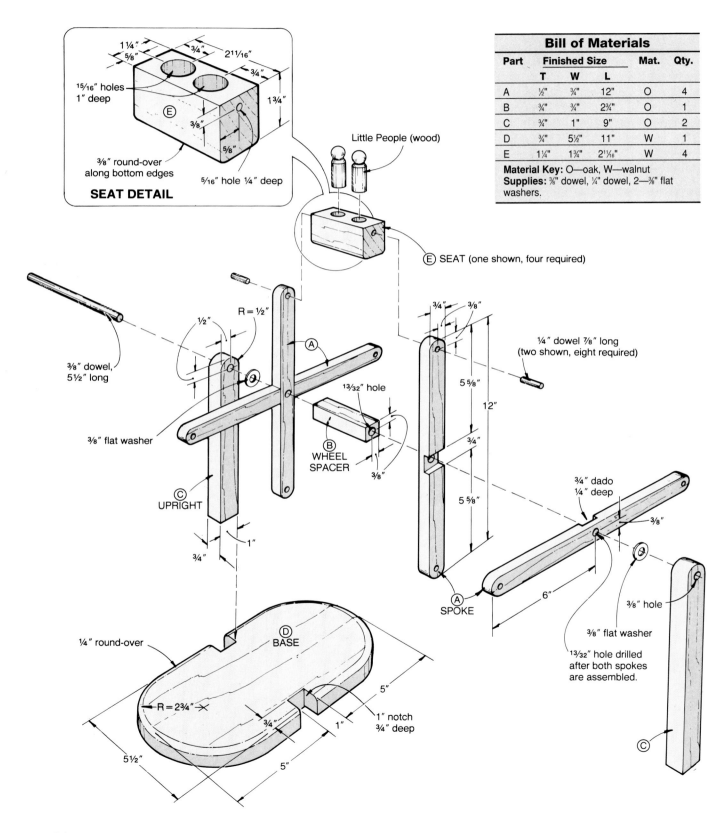

SEAT DETAIL

1¼″
⅝″
¾″
2¹¹⁄₁₆″
¾″
1¾″
¹⁵⁄₁₆″ holes 1″ deep
Ⓔ
⅜″
⅝″
⅜″ round-over along bottom edges
⁵⁄₁₆″ hole ¼″ deep

Bill of Materials				
Part	Finished Size		Mat.	Qty.
	T	W	L	
A	½″	¾″	12″	O	4
B	¾″	¾″	2¾″	O	1
C	¾″	1″	9″	O	2
D	¾″	5½″	11″	W	1
E	1¼″	1¾″	2¹¹⁄₁₆″	W	4

Material Key: O—oak, W—walnut
Supplies: ⅜″ dowel, ¼″ dowel, 2—⅜″ flat washers.

Little People (wood)

Ⓔ SEAT (one shown, four required)

⅜″ dowel, 5½″ long

R = ½″
½″
Ⓐ
⅜″ flat washer
Ⓒ UPRIGHT
¾″
1″

¹³⁄₃₂″ hole
Ⓑ WHEEL SPACER
⅜″

¾″
⅜″
5 ⅝″
12″
¾″
5 ⅝″
Ⓐ SPOKE

¼″ dowel ⅞″ long (two shown, eight required)

¾″ dado ¼″ deep
⅜″
6″
⅜″ hole
⅜″ flat washer
¹³⁄₃₂″ hole drilled after both spokes are assembled.
Ⓒ

¼″ round-over
Ⓓ BASE
R = 2¾″
¾″
5½″
5″
5″
1″
1″ notch ¾″ deep

Now, let's make the seats

1. Rip and crosscut a piece of walnut to 1¼x ¾x14". (If you don't have stock this thick, laminate two ¾" pieces together, and plane or resaw it to 1¼" thickness.)

2. Next, using a piloted ⅜" roundover bit in a table-mounted router, round-over the bottom edges of the piece. Finish-sand the piece.

3. Using dimensions in the Seat detail on the Exploded View drawing, crosscut the four seats (E) to length. Next, mark the location of the two 15/16" holes on the top edge, and the 5/16" holes on the ends of each seat. Drill the holes. (We used the jig shown *below* to position the piece and hold it square while drilling.) Finish sand all parts.

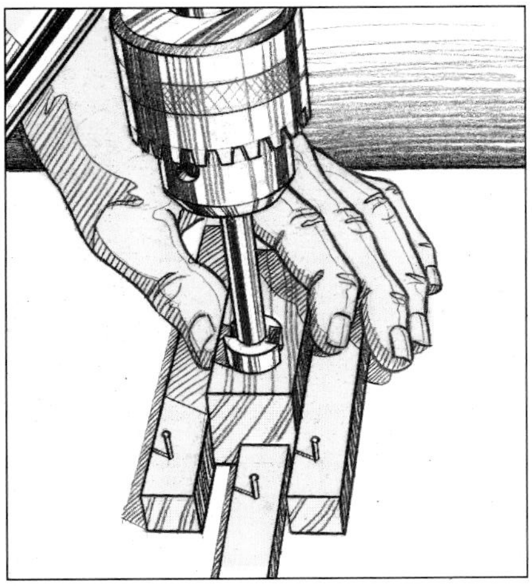

Time to assemble the wheel

1. Glue, assemble, and clamp both pairs of spokes at the half-lap joints. Square each pair at the corners. Wipe off any excess glue. After the glue dries, remove the clamps. Mark the centerpoint on each spoke set by striking crisscrossing lines from the spoke corners. Finally, drill a centered 13/32" hole through both lap-joints as shown *above, top right.*

2. Cut one 5½" length of ⅜" dowel for the wheel axle. Next, cut eight ¾" lengths of ¼" dowel for the seats. Glue one ¼" dowel in each of the eight holes at the ends of the wheel spokes.

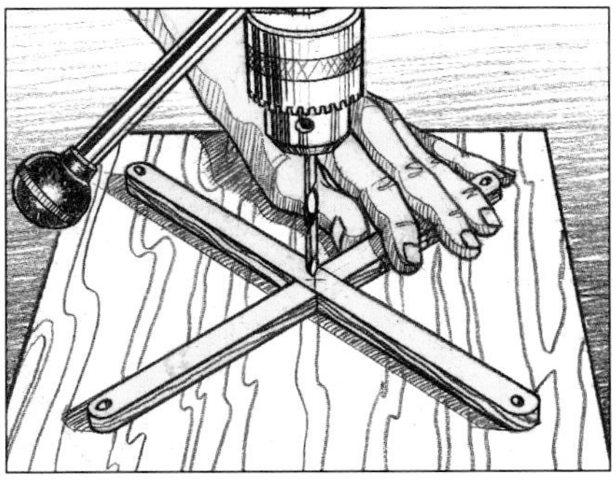

3. Lay one spoke set (outside face down) on a flat surface. Place the ⅜" axle dowel in the center hole. Apply glue to one end of the wheel spacer and slip it over the dowel. (Do not glue the dowel.) Let the assembly set until the glue dries.

4. Next, apply glue to the top end of the wheel spacer, then place the second spoke set over the axle dowel (outside face up) and onto the spacer. As you lower the top spoke set in place, position the seats on the ¼" dowels. Now, using a square as shown *below,* align opposing wheel spokes parallel to one another. When aligned, let the wheel set until the glue dries.

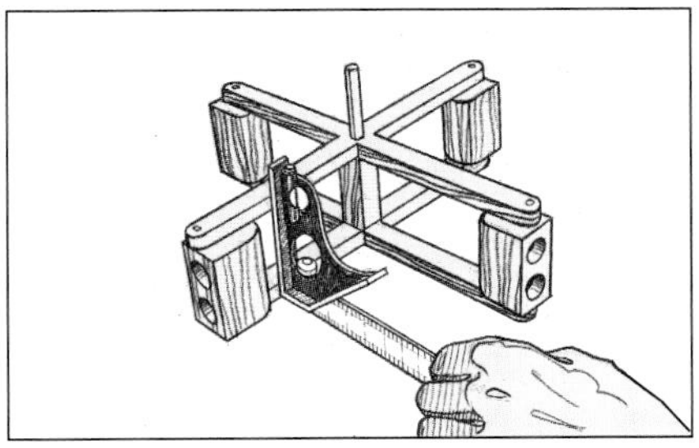

5. Remove the axle dowel from the wheel assembly and glue one end of it in the hole in one upright. Then, glue and clamp that upright in one of the two base notches. Let the glue dry, and remove the clamp. Now, from scrap, cut a spacer as long as the distance between the base notches.

6. Slip a ⅜" flat washer over the axle dowel, add the wheel assembly, and now add another washer. (We laid the assembly on its side for this.) Apply glue in the ⅜" hole of the second upright and in the remaining base notch. Place the upright's hole over the axle dowel and its bottom in the notch. Clamp the upright at the base. Place the spacer between the uprights (near the ends) and clamp. After the glue dries, remove the clamps and spacer.

7. Apply the finish of your choice. (We left the wood unstained and applied two coats of polyurethane.)

8. Finally, fill the Ferris wheel with Little People (see the Buying Guide for a source) and watch the eyes of those little ones light up. The wooden people come unfinished, but you can give them a lot of character with a few creative strokes of an artist's brush. (A Tole painter provided the finishing touches to ours, painting on faces, hair, arms, hands, and colorful clothing.)

Buying Guide

• **Little People.** Birch ⅞" diameter, 2¼" tall, unfinished. Cat. no. LP1. For current prices, contact Meisel Hardware Specialties, P.O. Box 70, Mound, MN 55364. Telephone 612-471-8550.

Project Tool List

Tablesaw
- Dado blade or dado set

Bandsaw

Disc/belt sander

Drill Press
- Bits: ¼", 5/16", ⅜", 13/32", 15/16"

Router
- Bits: ¼" round-over, ⅜" round-over

Finishing sander

Note: *We built the project using the tools listed. You may be able to substitute other tools or equipment for listed items you don't have. Additional common hand tools and clamps may be required to complete the project.*

ALPINE-RIDE ACTION TOY

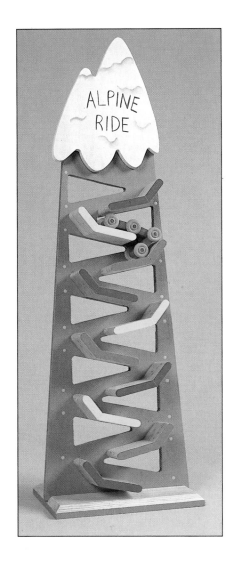

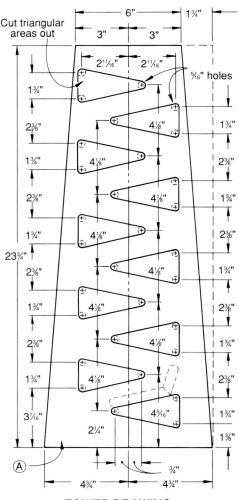

TOWER DRAWING

CUTTING DIAGRAM

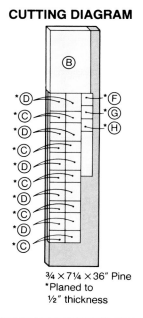

¾ × 7¼ × 36″ Pine
*Planed to
½″ thickness

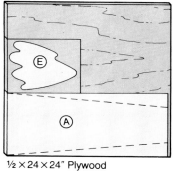

½ × 24 × 24″ Plywood

Create a thrill show for your favorite kids with this captivating toy. Just release the car at the top of the track and watch it race downhill, spilling from one level to the next. For easy storage, simply separate the tower from the base.

Make the tower first

1. Rip and crosscut a 12×24″ piece of ½″ plywood.

2. Scribe a light line lengthwise along the center of the plywood piece. Next, using the dimensions on the Tower drawing *above,*

center, and working from both the centerline and square bottom, lay out the tower (A) pattern on the plywood. Mark the centerpoints for the three ⁵⁄₁₆″ holes in each triangle cutout, the cutlines between the holes, the tapering tower sides, and the tower's final top and bottom.

3. Chuck a ⁵⁄₁₆″ bit in your drill press and drill the corner holes in each of the ten triangles where marked. (We placed scrap under the workpiece to avoid chip-out.)

4. Draw lines to connect the arcs of the three holes to form each triangle. Scrollsaw the triangles to

shape, cutting from the arc of one hole to the other, following the cutlines. Use a stiff saw blade to minimize blade deflection. Smooth the sawed edges with a wood rasp or file.

5. Saw the tower sides to shape. (We used our tablesaw and a taper jig set at 5°.) If you don't have a taper jig, you can saw the tower to shape on a bandsaw and sand the edges on a belt or disc sander.

6. For the base (B), rip and crosscut a piece of ¾″ stock to 6×9½″. (We used pine. See the Cutting Diagram *above.*) To cut the groove, mount a ½"-wide dado set to your tablesaw, angle the cutter to 8° from perpendicular, and then elevate it to cut a ⅜"-deep dado. Test the cutting depth on a piece of scrap. Now, dado the top surface of the base piece where shown. Mount your regular saw blade, angle it to 45°, and cut the ½" chamfer along the top edges of the base.

7. Finish-sand the tower and base pieces. If you plan to paint the tower as we did, paint it before you attach the ramps. (We painted the tower steel gray, and added yellow dots to represent rivets.)

Next, make the ramps and the top

1. To make the ramp pieces (C, D), rip two pieces of ¾" clear pine to 2¼x24". (See the Ramp detail at *right.*) Plane or resaw both pieces to ½" thickness. Sand if needed. Next, crosscut five 4⅝"-long ramp pieces from each length. Using your table-mounted router and a ¼" round-over bit, round over both ends on each of the 10 pieces.

2. To crosscut the ramp pieces, first place your miter gauge in the groove of your saw's table. Clamp a stop block to the gauge, 2¾" from the face of the saw blade. Angle your tablesaw blade to 15° from perpendicular. Now, one by one, place the pieces against the miter gauge and stop block, and bevel-crosscut them to make one C and one D from each.

3. Assemble the ramps by matching one C and one D piece together to make 10 pairs. Apply hot-melt glue to the beveled face of one piece as shown at *right,* and then join it to the beveled edge on its mating piece. Align and hold them together at that angle (30°) until the adhesive sets (about 15 seconds).

4. Using carbon paper or a photocopier, make a copy of the full-sized pattern of the top (E) on *page 71.* With spray adhesive, adhere the pattern to a 8x10" piece of ½" plywood. Using a bandsaw or

scrollsaw, cut the top to shape. Remove the pattern (we used lacquer thinner), and then finish-sand the top.

Cut out the car parts

1. Rip one piece of ¾" pine to 1¼x12". Plane or resaw the piece to ½" thickness.

continued

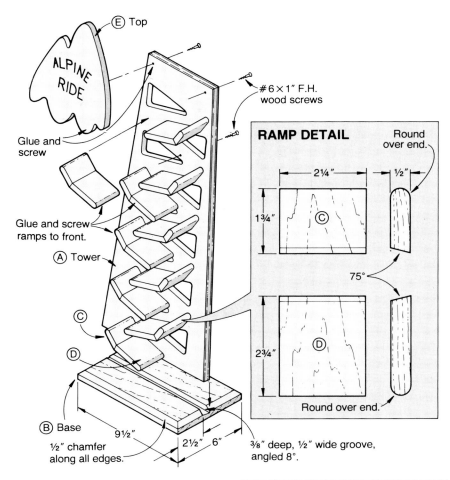

E Top

ALPINE RIDE

Glue and screw

Glue and screw ramps to front.

A Tower

C

D

B Base

½" chamfer along all edges.

9½"

2½" 6"

#6×1" F.H. wood screws

⅜" deep, ½" wide groove, angled 8°.

RAMP DETAIL

Round over end.

2¼" ½"

1¾" C

2¾" D

75°

Round over end.

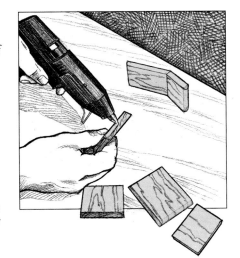

Bill of Materials					
Part	Finished Size*			Mat.	Qty.
	T	W	L		
A* tower	½"	9½"	23¾"	F	1
B base	¾"	6"	9½"	P	1
C ramp	½"	2¼"	1¾"	P	10
D ramp	½"	2¼"	2¾"	P	10
E* top	½"	8"	10"	F	1
F* car section	½"	1¼"	2"	P	1
G* car section	½"	1¼"	2"	P	1
H* car section	½"	1¼"	2"	P	1

* Parts marked with an * are cut to final size during construction.

Material Key: F—fir plywood; P—pine.
Supplies: ¼" dowel, 22-#6X1" flathead wood screws, 8¼X1" wood wheels, hot-melt glue, paint or finish.

ALPINE-RIDE ACTION TOY
continued

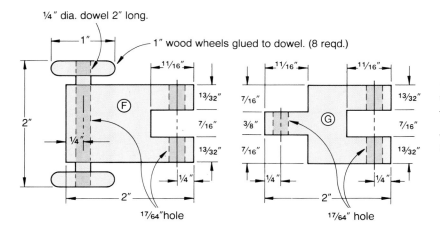

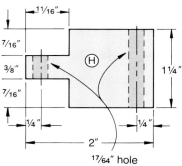

ALPINE CAR DETAIL

2. Using the dimensions on the Alpine Car drawing *above,* lay out the car sections (F, G, H) on the piece. Locate the hole centerlines, the tongues, and the slots on the top face. With a try square, transfer the six axle hole centerlines to one edge of the piece, find the edge's center, and then mark the hole centerpoints for the axle holes ¼" in from the ends of the sections.

3. Drill the axle holes through each car section. (We clamped the piece on edge in a handscrew clamp, centered one of the axle holes under the bit, and then clamped this assembly to the drill press table. We drilled each hole with a ¼" brad-point bit, then switched to a ¹⁷⁄₆₄" twist bit to enlarge them slightly.)

4. Crosscut the 12"-long piece where marked to form the three car sections (F, G, H). Using your bandsaw, cut the tongues on sections H and G, and the slots on F and G. (We used the saw's miter gauge and a scrap-wood support to ensure straight saw cuts.) Sand a roundover (we used our disc sander) on the ends on each car segment.

5. Cut four 2"-long lengths of ¼" diameter dowel for the car axles. Glue one end of each dowel in the hole of a 1"-diameter ¼"-thick wood wheel. (You'll find this size wheel frequently available at crafts supply

stores. Or, see the Buying Guide for a mail-order source.) Paint or finish the car sections before assembling.

Mount the ramps;
finish the assembly

1. To align the ramps, place a length of masking tape on the tower face along the outside edges of the triangles. Using hot-melt glue, adhere the ramps to the front of the tower, aligning the angled ends against the tapes, and the bottom edge of each with the top edge of the adjacent triangular opening.

2. Turn the tower and attached ramps facedown. Using a counter-sink/counterbore bit, drill two pilot holes through the tower and into each ramp. Drive two #6×1" flat-head wood screws into each. (We positioned the screws so one was driven into each ramp part.) Now, remove the tape.

3. Paint the top and any other parts you wish. (We painted the edge of the base [not the chamfer] gray to match the tower, and the front edges of the ramps red, yellow, and orange. We freehand-painted the name, and coated the unpainted wood parts with lacquer.)

4. After the paint has dried thoroughly, attach the top to the

tower with #6×1" flathead wood screws. (We drilled the screw pilot holes through the tower and into the back of the top.) Assemble the car sections and glue the wheels to the ends of the car axle dowels. Insert the bottom of the tower in the groove in the base so it leans backwards. Now, place the car on the top ramp and let it go.

Buying guide
• **Wood wheels.** 1" diam., ³⁄₁₆" thick, ¼" axle hole. Catalog no. W10020. For current prices contact Meisel Hardware Specialties, P.O. Box 70, Mound, MN 55364-0070.

Project Tool List
Tablesaw
    Dado blade or dado set
Scrollsaw
Drill press
    Bits: ¼", ¹⁷⁄₆₄", ⁵⁄₁₆"
Router
    Router table
    ¼" round-over bit
Finishing sander

Note: *We built the project using the tools listed. You may be able to substitute other tools or equipment for listed items you don't have. Additional common hand tools and clamps may be required to complete the project.*

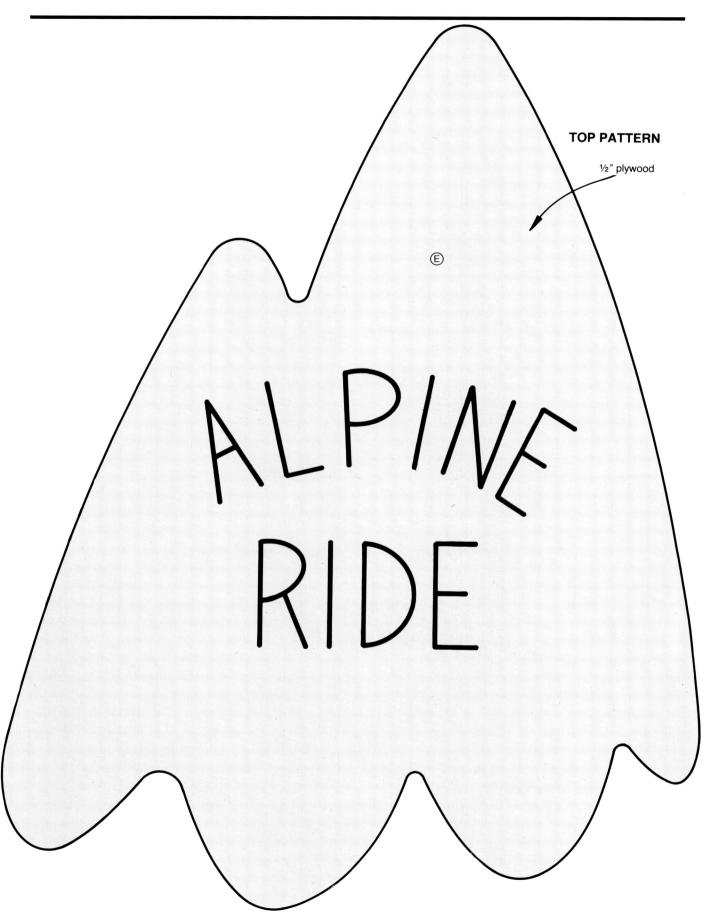

TOP PATTERN

½″ plywood

ⒺE

ALPINE RIDE

TEDDY BEAR MUSIC BOX

This adorable walnut bear, with its trio of colorful balloons, turns to the tune of "Music Box Dancer." To wind, just rotate the bear and turntable clockwise on the oak base. In the nursery or on the dresser, this project is a surefire heart-warmer.

Begin with the base block

1. Rip and crosscut two pieces of ¾" oak to 5½x5½" for the base block (A). Spread an even coat of glue onto the mating surfaces, and clamp the pieces face-to-face, with the grain going in the same direction on both pieces.

2. To finish forming the base block (A), follow the six-step Base Block drawing *opposite, top right.* See photo A *below right* for reference when forming the 2⅞"-diameter hole in the block.

3. Place the music movement in the 2⅞" hole in the base block. Now, center the movement's turntable shaft in the ½" hole in the base block. Hold the movement firmly in place, and poke a nail through the movement mounting holes and into the bottom face of the plug. Do this to make a slight indentation, marking the centerpoint for each of the three mounting screw holes.

4. Drill three ⅛" holes through the plug where indented with the nail. Then, working from the top side, center a 5⁄16" Forstner bit over each ⅛" mounting hole, and drill a counterbore ¼" deep (see the Section View *opposite* for reference).

The base bottom and turntable come next

1. Mark a 3" radius (6" circle) on a piece of ¾"-thick oak for the base bottom (C). Bandsaw the piece to shape, and sand the bandsawed edge smooth. (We bandsawed just outside the marked line, and then sanded to the line with a disc sander.)

A Use a circle cutter to form the 2⅞" hole in the laminated base block.

B Cut the recess for the plastic turntable in the wood turntable (D).

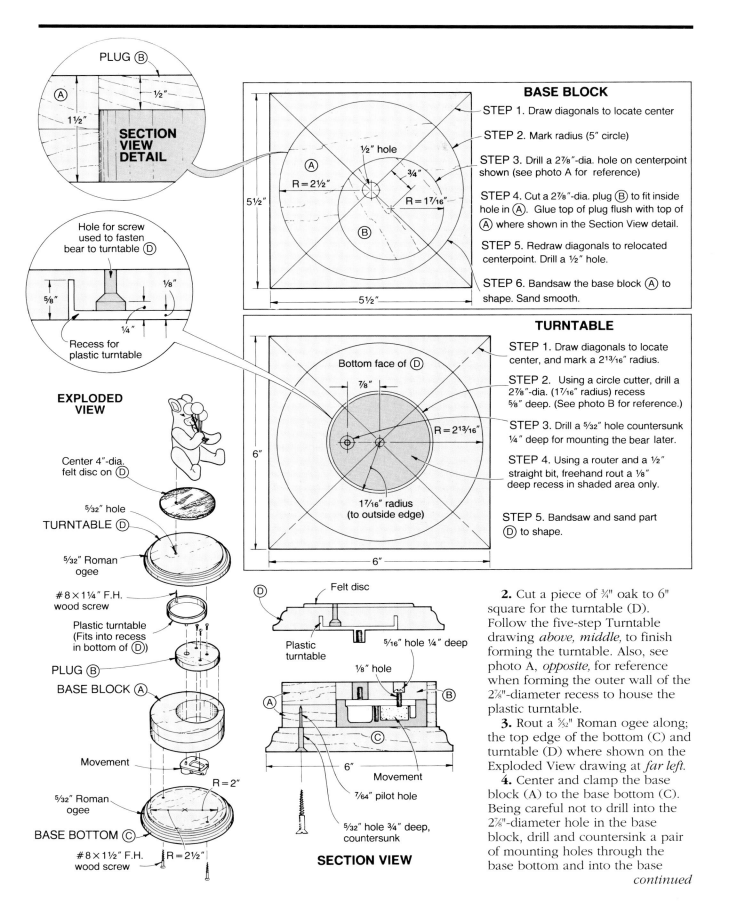

SECTION VIEW DETAIL

PLUG (B)

(A)

1½″

½″

BASE BLOCK

STEP 1. Draw diagonals to locate center

STEP 2. Mark radius (5″ circle)

STEP 3. Drill a 2⅞″-dia. hole on centerpoint shown (see photo A for reference)

STEP 4. Cut a 2⅞″-dia. plug (B) to fit inside hole in (A). Glue top of plug flush with top of (A) where shown in the Section View detail.

STEP 5. Redraw diagonals to relocated centerpoint. Drill a ½″ hole.

STEP 6. Bandsaw the base block (A) to shape. Sand smooth.

½″ hole

(A)

R = 2½″

¾″

R = 1⁷⁄₁₆″

(B)

5½″

5½″

Hole for screw used to fasten bear to turntable (D)

⅝″

⅛″

¼″

Recess for plastic turntable

TURNTABLE

STEP 1. Draw diagonals to locate center, and mark a 2¹³⁄₁₆″ radius.

STEP 2. Using a circle cutter, drill a 2⅞″-dia. (1⁷⁄₁₆″ radius) recess ⅝″ deep. (See photo B for reference.)

STEP 3. Drill a 5⁄32″ hole countersunk ¼″ deep for mounting the bear later.

STEP 4. Using a router and a ½″ straight bit, freehand rout a ⅛″ deep recess in shaded area only.

STEP 5. Bandsaw and sand part (D) to shape.

Bottom face of (D)

⅞″

R = 2¹³⁄₁₆″

6″

1⁷⁄₁₆″ radius (to outside edge)

6″

EXPLODED VIEW

Center 4″-dia. felt disc on (D)

5⁄32″ hole

TURNTABLE (D)

5⁄32″ Roman ogee

#8 × 1¼″ F.H. wood screw

Plastic turntable (Fits into recess in bottom of (D))

PLUG (B)

BASE BLOCK (A)

Movement

5⁄32″ Roman ogee

BASE BOTTOM (C)

#8 × 1½″ F.H. wood screw

R = 2″

R = 2½″

SECTION VIEW

(D)

Felt disc

Plastic turntable

5⁄16″ hole ¼″ deep

⅛″ hole

(A)

(B)

(C)

6″

Movement

7⁄64″ pilot hole

5⁄32″ hole ¾″ deep, countersunk

2. Cut a piece of ¾″ oak to 6″ square for the turntable (D). Follow the five-step Turntable drawing *above, middle,* to finish forming the turntable. Also, see photo A, *opposite,* for reference when forming the outer wall of the 2⅞″-diameter recess to house the plastic turntable.

3. Rout a 5⁄32″ Roman ogee along; the top edge of the bottom (C) and turntable (D) where shown on the Exploded View drawing at *far left.*

4. Center and clamp the base block (A) to the base bottom (C). Being careful not to drill into the 2⅞″-diameter hole in the base block, drill and countersink a pair of mounting holes through the base bottom and into the base

continued

TEDDY BEAR MUSIC BOX
continued

block. See the Section View drawing for reference and hole sizes.

5. Sand the top surface of the plastic turntable, and epoxy it into the recess on the bottom of the turntable (D).

The bear facts

1. From ¾" walnut, cut one block for the body (E), two blocks for the front legs (F), and two blocks for the back legs (G) to the sizes shown on the full-sized patterns.

2. From ½" walnut stock, cut the two ear pieces (H) to the sizes listed on the full-sized patterns.

3. Using carbon paper or a photocopy and spray adhesive, transfer the Side View Body pattern for parts (E, F, G, H) to the blocks of wood cut in Step 1.

4. Following the pattern lines and using either a bandsaw or a scrollsaw, cut the legs and body parts.

5. Next, mark the bevel location on each leg, and sand to the line. (We shaped the bevels on a stationary belt sander.)

6. Drill a ⁷⁄₆₄" pilot hole ¾" deep in the bottom of the bear body (E) where shown on the full sized pattern at *right*.

7. Rout or sand ¼" round-overs on all *but the mating edges* of the four legs and body where shown on the Bear drawing. (To keep our fingers safely away from the router bit, we held the pieces in a small handscrew clamp when routing as shown in the drawing *opposite*. We had to change the clamp's position on each body part several times to rout all the required areas.)

8. Glue the legs and ears to the bear body where indicated on the body pattern at *right* (we held

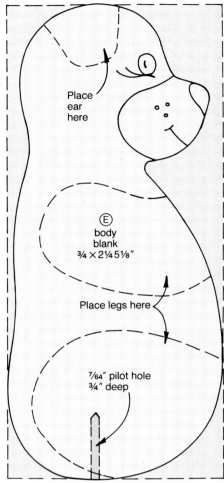

Place ear here

Ⓔ body blank ¾ × 2¼ 5⅛"

Place legs here

⁷⁄₆₄" pilot hole ¾" deep

the pieces in place with spring clamps until the glue dried; masking tape also works well).

Let's add the balloons

1. Holding the right front leg in a handscrew clamp, drill ¼" balloon dowel holes where shown on the Side View Front Legs pattern. Finish-sand the leg.

2. Drill a ⅛" hole ¼" deep in three 1"-diameter wooden balls.

3. Cut six pieces of ⅛" dowel stock to the lengths listed on the Bear drawing at *left*. Glue the three longer pieces into the ⅛" holes in the balloons.

4. Using the dowels as handles, paint the three wooden balls. Next, glue the balloon dowels into the top ¼" hole in the bear's right-front leg. Later, glue the three shorter dowels into the opposite end of the hole.

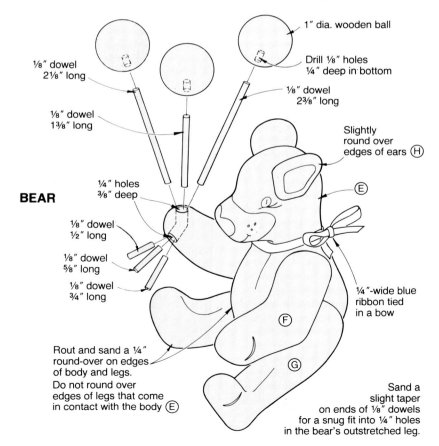

1" dia. wooden ball

⅛" dowel 2⅛" long

⅛" dowel 1⅜" long

Drill ⅛" holes ¼" deep in bottom

⅛" dowel 2⅜" long

Slightly round over edges of ears Ⓗ

BEAR

¼" holes ⅜" deep

⅛" dowel ½" long

⅛" dowel ⅝" long

⅛" dowel ¾" long

Ⓔ

¼"-wide blue ribbon tied in a bow

Ⓕ

Ⓖ

Rout and sand a ¼" round-over on edges of body and legs. Do not round over edges of legs that come in contact with the body Ⓔ

Sand a slight taper on ends of ⅛" dowels for a snug fit into ¼" holes in the bear's outstretched leg.

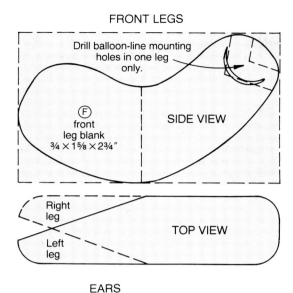

FRONT LEGS

Drill balloon-line mounting holes in one leg only.

F
front leg blank
$\frac{3}{4} \times 1\frac{5}{8} \times 2\frac{3}{4}$"

SIDE VIEW

Right leg

Left leg

TOP VIEW

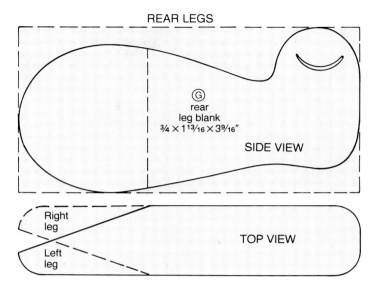

REAR LEGS

G
rear leg blank
$\frac{3}{4} \times 1\frac{13}{16} \times 3\frac{9}{16}$"

SIDE VIEW

Right leg

Left leg

TOP VIEW

EARS

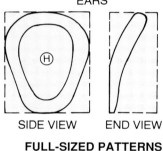

H

SIDE VIEW   END VIEW

FULL-SIZED PATTERNS

ROUTING ROUND-OVER ON LEGS

Do not rout these edges

Sand and apply the finish

1. Sand slight round-overs on the ears. Then, finish-sand all the bear and box parts. Remove the movement from the base block, and apply finish to all the parts.

2. Paint the mouth/muzzle area, and eyes where shown on the body pattern *opposite* and opening

photograph. (We used model-airplane enamels.)

3. Cut a 4"-diameter piece of felt. With 150-grit sandpaper, rough up the finish where the pieces mate. Center and glue the felt to the top of the turntable. Equally space and tap three thumbtacks into the top of the base block where shown on the Exploded View drawing.

4. Fasten the bear to the turntable, and add the bow to the bear.

5. Stick the threaded shaft through the hole, and fasten the movement to the base block with three mounting screws. Screw the base bottom to the bottom of the base block with a pair of screws.

6. Center the shaft from the plastic turntable over the threaded shaft protruding from the music movement and partially through the $\frac{1}{2}$" hole in the plug (B). Slowly rotate the turntable/bear clockwise to thread the assembly onto the movement shaft.

Note: Be careful not to overwind the mechanism ($2\frac{1}{2}$ revolutions is sufficient). After winding the music box, there should be about a $\frac{1}{2}$" gap between the base block (A) and the turntable (D). If the turntable winds tightly against the base block, remove the movement from the base block, and belt-sand the top of the block to remove a bit of stock. If the turntable winds tightly against the

base block, the music movement won't play and the turntable won't turn.

Buying Guide

• **Music box kit.** Hand-crafted Swiss Reuge 18-note music movement playing "Music Box Dancer," plastic turntable for movement, and three 1" wooden balls (for balloons). Kit no. 71101. For current prices contact Klockit, P.O. Box 636, Lake Geneva, WI 53147. Or, call 800-556-2548 to order.

Project Tool List

Tablesaw
Bandsaw
Scrollsaw
Belt sander
Drill press
  Bits: $\frac{7}{64}$", $\frac{1}{8}$", $\frac{5}{32}$", $\frac{1}{4}$", $\frac{5}{16}$", $\frac{1}{2}$"
  Drum sander
  Circle cutter
Router
  Router table
  Bits: $\frac{5}{32}$" Roman ogee, $\frac{1}{4}$" round-over, $\frac{1}{2}$" straight
Finishing sander

Note: We built the project using the tools listed. You may be able to substitute other tools or equipment for listed items you don't have. Additional common hand tools and clamps may be required to complete the project.

ONE LEAN JELLY BEAN MACHINE

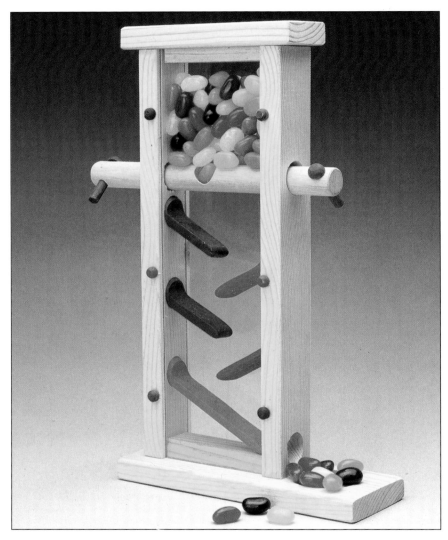

centered from edge to edge, on the inside face of the two sidepieces. Now, as shown *below*, tilt the table on your drill press table 30° from center. (If your table doesn't tilt, make a temporary jig to hold the sidepieces at the desired angle and clamp it in place while you drill the holes.) Using a brad-point bit, carefully drill 1" holes ⅜" deep for the slides, making sure you angle each hole as shown on the Side View drawing. (We set the stop on our drill press to prevent drilling through the side, and then test-drilled holes in scrap stock.) Next, drill completely through the right hand sidepiece for the angled-exit hole.

4. Level the drill press table, and the 1" hole in each sidepiece (where marked) for the crank. Now, drill a 2"-diameter hole ⅜" deep, centered from side to side, in the base where located on the Side View drawing. (We used a Forstner bit.)

5. Cut two pieces of ⅛" clear acrylic to 4½x13" long. (We cut ours on a bandsaw fitted with a ⅛" fine-tooth blade but you can use a tablesaw.) Leave the protective cover on the acrylic to avoid scratching the surfaces until you're ready to install the panels.

6. To form the four short slides (E) shown in the Exploded View

This clever, fun-to-build project not only fascinates, it also satisfies your sweet tooth in a hurry. Just fill it with jelly beans, turn the crank, and watch your treat tumble down the slides and into your hand.

First, let's cut the parts

1. Rip and crosscut the sides (A), the cover pieces (B, C), and the base pieces (C, D) to the sizes listed in the Bill of Materials

opposite. (We made our jelly bean machine out of ¾" pine.)

2. Cut a ⅛" saw kerf ½" deep and ³⁄₁₆" in from the outside edges of each sidepiece where shown on the Exploded View drawing *opposite.* (These kerfs hold the clear acrylic panels.)

3. Using the dimensions on the Side View drawing, *opposite,* mark the center point locations for the five dowel slides (E, F), the two 1" crank holes, and the exit hole

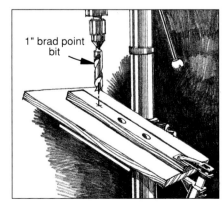

1" brad point bit

drawing, first cut a piece of 1"-diameter dowel stock to 11" long. Then, cut a piece of scrap to 3X4". Position the dowel on scrap so each end extends 3½" beyond the ends (see at *right)*.

7. Snip off the head of a 4-penny nail, and use the nail as a bit to drill two holes through the dowel and into the scrap holder. Nail the dowel to the holder.

8. Using the Full-Sized Slide drawing on *page 78* as a pattern, mark cutlines on each end of the dowel where shown. (We traced two patterns on paper and adhered one to each end of the dowel with spray adhesive.) Then, using a bandsaw fitted with a ⅛" blade, cut the curved lines first. Then, crosscut the slides to length where shown with the dotted line. (You'll get two slides from each end of the dowel.)

9. To form the longer bottom slide, cut a 1"-diameter dowel to 9". Then use the full-sized drawing of F and the ¾" scrap holder, and repeat steps 7 and 8.

10. Cut the crank (G) to length from 1" dowel stock. (We sanded the dowel so it would turn easily in the 1" hole.) Drill a ¾" hole ½" deep at the center. Next, drill a ⅜" hole ½" from each end of the dowel crank. (We held the dowel crank in a handscrew when drilling the holes. If you have a V-block jig, that will also work.)

continued

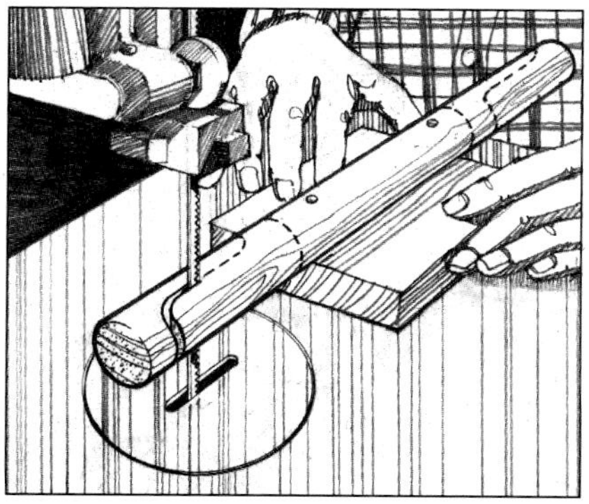

SIDE VIEW

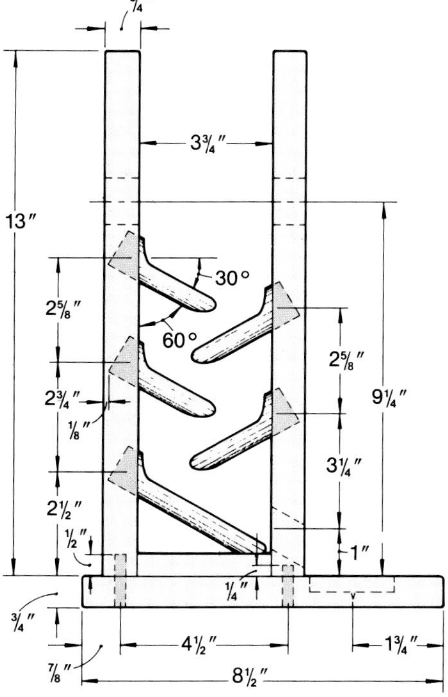

3/4″
3 3/4″
13″
30°
2 5/8″
60°
2 5/8″
2 3/4″
1/8″
9 1/4″
3 1/4″
2 1/2″
1/2″
1″
1/4″
3/4″
4 1/2″
1 3/4″
7/8″
8 1/2″

EXPLODED VIEW

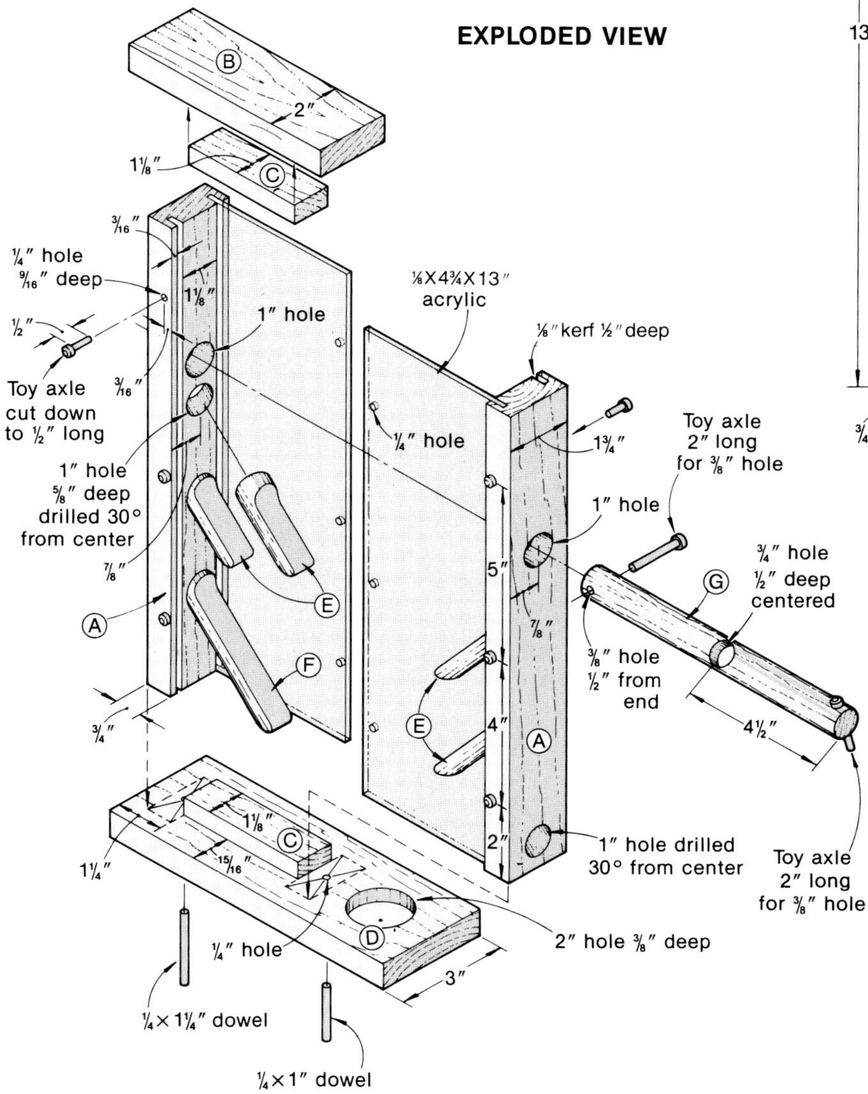

B
2″
1 1/8″
C
3/16″
1/4″ hole
9/16″ deep
1 1/8″
1″ hole
1/2″
Toy axle cut down to 1/2″ long
3/16″
1″ hole
5/8″ deep
drilled 30° from center
7/8″
A
E
F
3/4″
1/8X4 3/4X13″ acrylic
1/8″kerf 1/2″deep
1/4″ hole
1 3/4″
Toy axle 2″ long for 3/8″ hole
1″ hole
5″
7/8″
G
3/4″ hole
1/2″ deep
centered
3/8″ hole
1/2″ from end
E
4″
A
4 1/2″
2″
1″ hole drilled 30° from center
Toy axle 2″ long for 3/8″ hole
1 1/4″
1 1/8″
C
15/16″
1/4″ hole
D
2″ hole 3/8″ deep
3″
1/4 × 1 1/4″ dowel
1/4 × 1″ dowel

Bill of Materials

Part	Finished Size* T	W	L	Mat.	Qty.
A	¾"	1¾"	13"	P	2
B	¾"	2"	6"	P	1
C	½"	1⅛"	3$^{11}/_{16}$"	P	2
D	¾"	2¾"	8½"	P	1
E*	1" dia.		2¾"	BD	4
F*	1" dia.		4½"	BD	1
G	1" dia.		9"	BD	1

* Parts marked with an * are cut larger initially, and then trimmed to finished size. Please read the instructions before cutting.

Material Key: P—pine, BD—birch dowel
Supplies: 12—toy axle pegs for ¼" holes, 2—toy axle pegs for ⅜" holes, 2 pieces of ⅛X4¾X13" acrylic, ¼" dowel stock, marking pens or analine dyes for coloring parts.

ONE LEAN JELLY BEAN MACHINE
continued

SLIDES FULL-SIZE

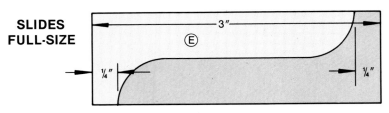

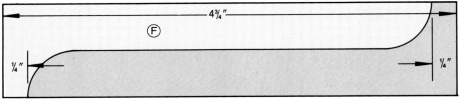

Now, assemble and finish the dispenser

1. Use red, green, and blue felt-tipped marking pens or analine dyes to color the slides.

2. Glue the slides into their respective holes, wiping off excess glue squeeze-out with a damp cloth.

3. Center the smaller of the cover pieces (C) on the bottom face of the larger cover piece (B). Mark the location of C on B, apply glue to the top face of C, and glue and clamp it to the area just marked.

4. Glue and clamp the base pieces (C, D) together (see the Exploded View drawing on *page 77* for positioning). If necessary, trim part C to fit between the saw kerfs in the sidepieces.

5. Position the acrylic panels in the kerfs between the sidepieces. With the ends of the acrylic flush with the ends of the sidepieces, "clamp" the assembly together with tape or rubber bands. To hold the acrylic panels permanently in place, use a brad-point bit to drill ¼" holes ⁵⁄₁₆" from the inside edge of both sidepieces where indicated on the Exploded View drawing.

6. Stain or use felt-tipped marking pens to color the twelve ¼" and two ⅜" toy axle pegs. Cut the shanks of the ¼" axles down to ½" long. Apply a dab of glue to the tip and insert the toy axles to peg the acrylic panels in position. You can buy toy axle pegs from many mail-order suppliers.

7. Position the slide assembly on the base and over part C. Trace the outline of the bottom ends of the sidepieces on the top face of the base (D). Remove the slide assembly. Draw diagonals in each marked rectangular outline to find the center. Now drill a ¼" hole through the base at the center of each diagonal. Reposition the slide assembly on the base, and using the ¼" holes you just drilled in the base as guides, drill ½" deep into the end of the lefthand sidepiece and ¼" deep into the righthand sidepiece as dimensioned on the Side View drawing.

8. From ¼"-diameter dowel stock, cut one piece to 1¼" long and another to 1" long. Glue and dowel the slide assembly to the base. Hand-sand the wood pieces smooth, sanding a slight roundover on all edges. Finish as desired. (We applied spray lacquer.)

9. Slide the crank into position, and install a ⅜" axle peg at each end of it. Now, fill the hopper, turn the crank, and watch the candy tumble down.

Project Tool List
Tablesaw
Bandsaw
Drill press
   Bits: ¼", ⅜", ¾", 1", 2"
Finishing sander

Note: We built the project using the tools listed. You may be able to substitute other tools or equipment for listed items you don't have. Additional common hand tools and clamps may be required to complete the project.

FUN-TIME TOTE BOX

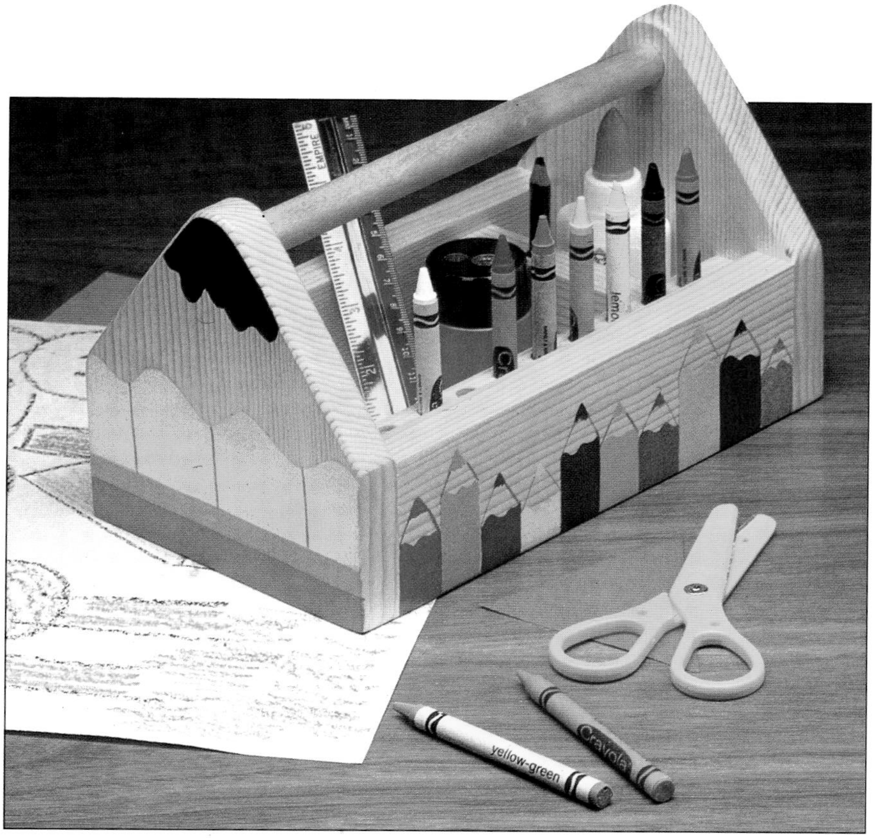

A place for everything, and everything in its place—that describes this easy-to-build child pleaser. Drilled holes and compartments create storage for crayons, pencils, scissors, glue, and other art necessities. And, a convenient dowel handle enables your budding Picasso to tote his or her tools of the trade from place to place.

Cut the box parts

1. Rip and crosscut a piece of ¾" pine to 5⅜x12". See the Cutting Diagram on *page 80.*

2. Photocopy or trace two copies of the end (A) patterns (on *page 80*), cut them to shape, and adhere both to the pine board. (We used spray adhesive for this.)

3. Bandsaw the two end pieces to shape. (We cut outside the line, and then sanded to the line.)

4. Make the sides (B), sawing two pieces of ¾" stock to the dimensions listed in the Bill of Materials. Using your tablesaw, cut a ⅜" rabbet ¼" deep along the bottom edge of each side piece.

5. Using a ¼" round-over bit, rout the end pieces where shown on the Exploded View drawing on *page 80.* Bore the ⅝" handle hole ⅜" deep on the inside face of each end. Drill the ¼" holes through each piece. Now, remove the paper patterns.

6. Rip and crosscut a piece of ¾" pine to 2x8" for the crayon strip (C), and one piece to 2x3⅛" for the divider (D).

7. Lay out the ⅜" holes centered along the top edge of the crayon strip and divider, using dimensions on the Exploded View. Drill the holes 1⅜" deep as shown at *right.*

8. From ¼" plywood, rip and crosscut the box bottom (E) to the dimensions listed in the Bill of Materials on *page 80.* Cut eight ¼" dowels and one ⅝" dowel to the indicated lengths. Finish-sand all parts.

Next, assemble the box

1. Glue and nail (we used yellow woodworker's glue and 4d finish nails) the divider piece 1¼" from one end of the crayon strip. See the Exploded View drawing for details. Glue and clamp this assembly to a side piece, aligning the parts with the top edge of the rabbet that you cut along the bottom of the side where shown.

2. Clamp the second side piece vertically in your bench vise. Place one of the end pieces on it and align the edges. With a ¼" bit, drill through the existing holes in the end piece and ⅞" deep into the side piece as shown on *page 80.* (We set a depth gauge on the drill bit at 1½" plus ⅛" to allow for the glue.)

3. Apply glue in the holes and run a bead of glue along the end of the side piece. Next, put the end in place and tap in two ¼" dowels (chamfered ends in) to secure the end to the side. Reverse this assembly in the vise, place the

continued

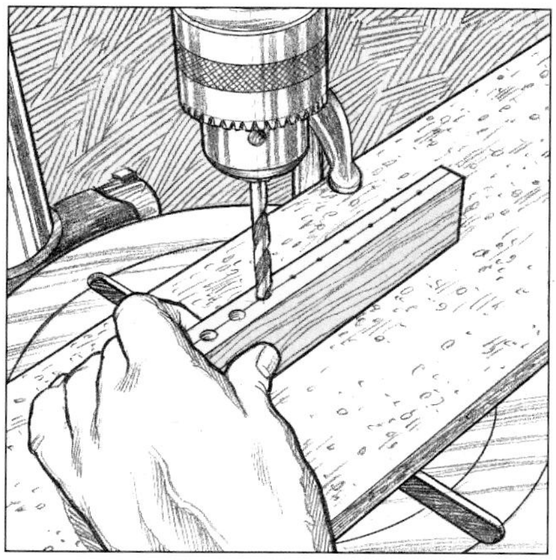

FUN-TIME TOTE BOX

continued

Bill of Materials

Part	Finished Size*			Mat.	Qty.
	T	W	L		
A* ends	¾"	5⅜"	5⅝"	P	2
B sides	¾"	2½"	8"	P	2
C crayon strip	¾"	2"	8"	P	1
D divider	¾"	2"	3⅛"	P	1
E bottom	¼"	4⅝"	8"	F	1
F handle	⅝"dia.		8¾"	B	1

*Parts cut to size during construction.

Material Key: P—pine, F—fir plywood, B—birch dowel (⅝" diameter).
Supplies: ¼" dowel, 1"X17 nails, water-based varnish, acrylic paints.

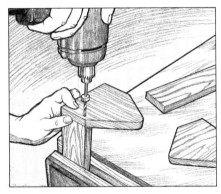

other end on the end of the side piece, and repeat the drilling process (as in step 2). Remove the assembly from the vise.

4. Clamp the side and crayon strip assembly vertically in your vise. Place the end and side assembly you made in step 3 on top, align edges, and then drill the ¼" holes through the end piece and into the side as you did earlier. Next, glue and dowel the side/crayon strip assembly to the end. (We clamped a 1¼"-wide spacer between the end and divider while the glue dried.)

5. Place the completed end of the assembly on your workbench. Apply glue in the ⅝" hole and insert one end of the ⅝" dowel. Next, apply glue to all mating edges, and in the ⅝" hole

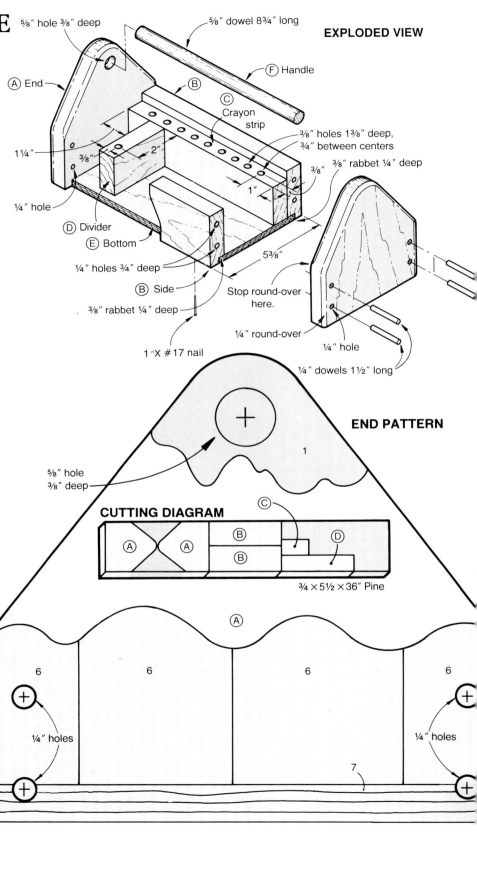

in the second end piece. Place that end on the assembly, inserting the free end of the ⅜" dowel into the hole. Align the edges, and then tap dowels into the holes already drilled. Drill the remaining two holes into the other side, and glue in those dowels. Square the box and clamp it (we used bar clamps) until dry. Sand the dowels flush with the face of the ends.

6. Glue and nail the bottom into the side rabbets and between the ends. (We used 1"x17 nails.)

Finish it with color

1. Seal all surfaces. (We applied one coat of water-based varnish [from a crafts supply store], let it dry, and sanded it with 220-grit sandpaper.)

2. Transfer the painting patterns *right,* onto the sides of the box, and the large pencil pattern onto the ends of the box. (We copied the patterns onto tracing paper with a #2 pencil. Next, we flipped the patterns, centered and aligned them along the box bottom, and taped them in place. We then traced over the lines with a ballpoint pen to transfer the carbon onto the wood.)

3. Now, using a fine brush, paint the crayons and pencils following our color key or your own color scheme. (We used Delta brand Ceramcoat acrylic paints.) Once dry, apply a second sealer coat.

Project Tool List
Tablesaw
Bandsaw
Disc sander
Portable drill
Drill press
  Bits: ¼", ⅜", ⅝"
Router
  ¼" round-over bit
Finishing sander

Note: We built the project using the tools listed. You may be able to substitute other tools or equipment for listed items you don't have. Additional common hand tools and clamps may be required to complete the project.

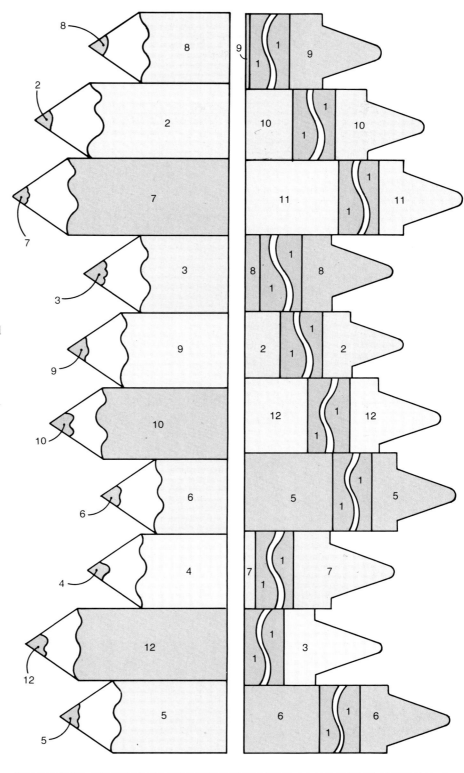

Color Key			
1. Black	**4** Red	**7.** Gray	**10.** Dark green
2. Dark blue	**5.** Orange	**8.** Light green	**11.** Purple
3. Light blue	**6.** Yellow	**9.** Pink	**12.** Aquamarine

ARMORED-CAR BANK

Encourage a child to save by parking this handsome vehicle on his or her dresser. Made from walnut and maple, our armored-car bank offers ample storage for bills and change. A padlocked door at the rear opens with a key, allowing for rainy-day withdrawals.

Start by building the car chassis

1. Using a photocopier or carbon paper, copy the full-sized patterns on *pages 84–85.* Cut out the pattern copies with scissors, leaving a margin around the outlines.

2. Laminate three ⅜×5½×24" pieces together face to face. (We used walnut.) After squaring the lamination, rip and crosscut one 4½×10½" piece from it. Apply spray adhesive on the back of pattern A and glue it to the edge of the piece. (We aligned the bottom of the pattern with the bottom of the piece.) Saw the chassis (A) to shape

on your bandsaw as shown *below.* Remove the pattern.

3. Using a penny for the form, scribe a ⅜" radius on all four corners of the chassis. Cut the radii to shape on your bandsaw, and sand.

4. Rout a ¼" round-over on the chassis fenders where shown on the Exploded View drawing

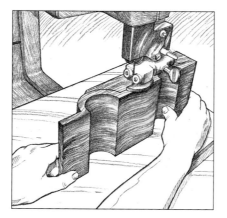

opposite. Hand-sand where the fenders meet the running boards.

5. Rip and crosscut a 1¾×2¾" block from the 2¼"-thick lamination. Adhere axle pattern B to the edge. Cut a second block to 3¼×2¾" from the lamination. Adhere axle pattern C to the edge of it. Drill an ¹¹⁄₃₂" hole ¾" deep in both ends of both parts where indicated on the pattern. (We used a Stanley 59 Doweling Jig when drilling to ensure the axle holes align at both ends on each block.)

6. Saw both axles to shape on your bandsaw. Next, test-fit the axles in the wheel wells of the chassis. Sand the parts to adjust the fit if necessary. Remove the patterns, center, glue, and clamp both parts (we used woodworkers' glue) in the wheel wells of the chassis.

Next, make the body

1. Rip and crosscut a piece of ¾" maple stock to 5½×30". Plane or resaw the piece to ⅜" thick.

2. From the ⅜" maple, crosscut two 6½"-long pieces for the car body sides (D). Rip both pieces to a width of 3⅛". Using double-faced tape, stick the two pieces together face to face, and adhere pattern D to the top piece. Cut the parts to shape, using a bandsaw. Sand the cut edges. Separate the pieces, and remove the tape and pattern.

3. To form the engine hood (E), rip and crosscut a 3½×2⅞" block from the 2¼" lamination. Stick pattern E to the edge. Bandsaw the wheel well. Test-fit the hood and body parts together on the chassis. Sand the parts to fit if necessary. Now, following the pattern line, saw the top of the hood to shape. Finish-sand the hood, sides, and the exposed parts of the chassis. Finally, sand a round-over on the five exposed edges of the hood.

4. Rip and crosscut a piece of ⅜" maple to 2¾×3" for the door (F). Cut two ⅜"-wide strips of thin

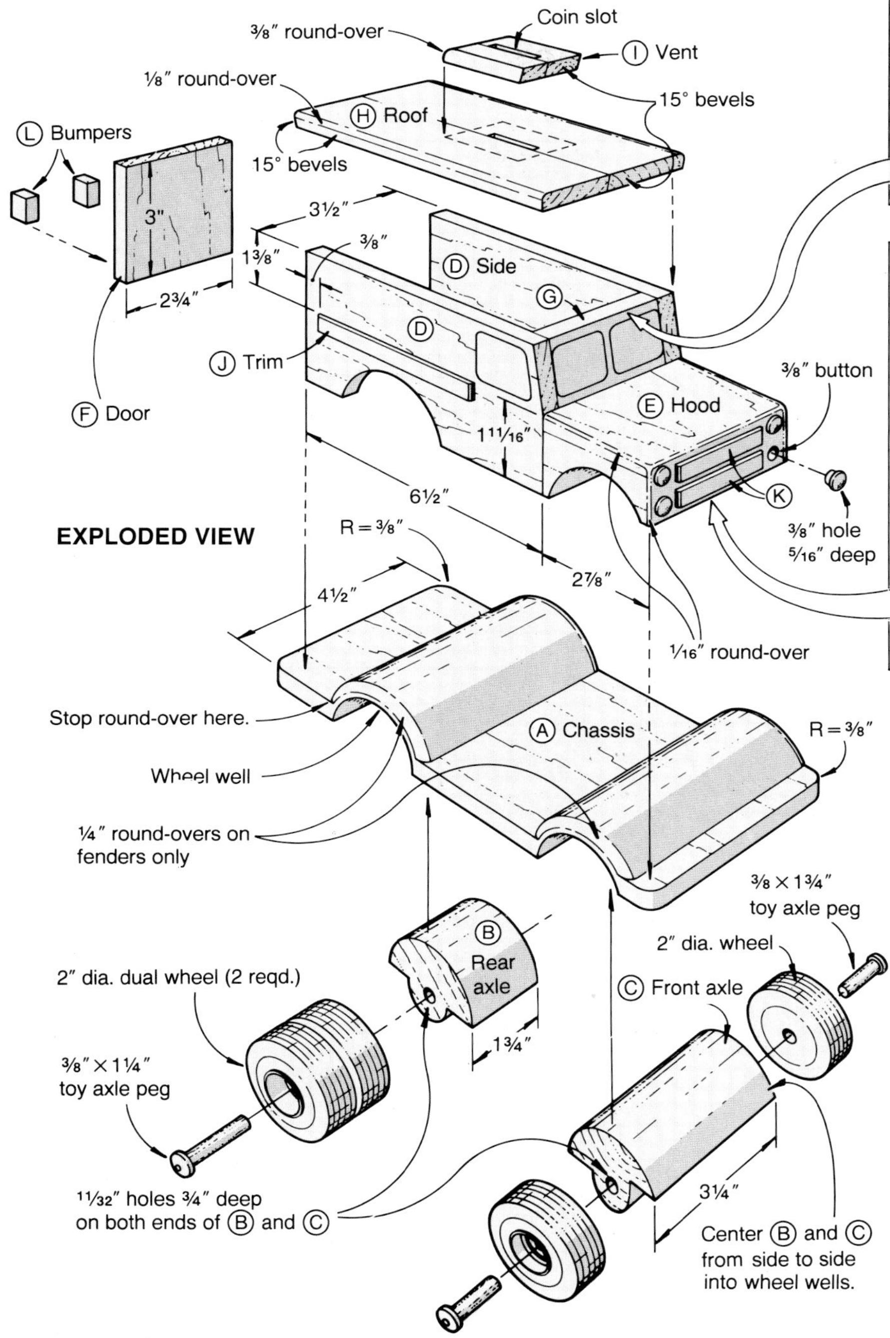
EXPLODED VIEW
Coin slot
3/8" round-over
Ⓘ Vent
1/8" round-over
Ⓗ Roof
15° bevels
15° bevels
Ⓛ Bumpers
3"
2 3/4"
3 1/2"
1 3/8"
3/8"
Ⓓ Side
Ⓖ
Ⓓ
Ⓙ Trim
Ⓕ Door
Ⓔ Hood
3/8" button
1 11/16"
Ⓚ
3/8" hole
5/16" deep
6 1/2"
R = 3/8"
2 7/8"
4 1/2"
1/16" round-over
Stop round-over here.
Ⓐ Chassis
R = 3/8"
Wheel well
1/4" round-overs on
fenders only
3/8 × 1 3/4"
toy axle peg
2" dia. wheel
Ⓑ
Rear
axle
Ⓒ Front axle
2" dia. dual wheel (2 reqd.)
1 3/4"
3/8" × 1 1/4"
toy axle peg
3 1/4"
11/32" holes 3/4" deep
on both ends of Ⓑ and Ⓒ
Center Ⓑ and Ⓒ
from side to side
into wheel wells.

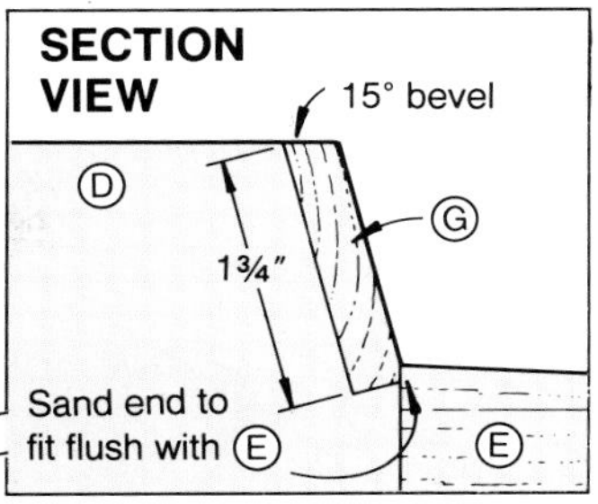
SECTION
VIEW
15° bevel
Ⓓ
Ⓖ
1 3/4"
Sand end to
fit flush with Ⓔ
Ⓔ

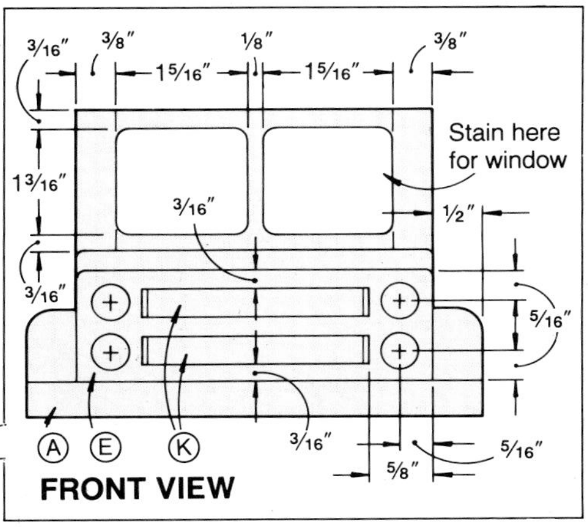
3/16"
3/8"
1 5/16"
1/8"
1 5/16"
3/8"
Stain here
for window
1 3/16"
3/16"
1/2"
3/16"
5/16"
Ⓐ Ⓔ Ⓚ
3/16"
5/8"
5/16"
FRONT VIEW

Part	Finished Size* T	W	L	Mat.	Qty.
A	1½"	4½"	10¼"	W	1
B	1⅝"	2¼"	1¾"	W	1
C	1⅝"	2³⁄₁₆"	3¼"	W	1
D	⅜"	3⅛"	6½"	M	2
E	1¹¹⁄₁₆"	3½"	2⅞"	W	1
F	⅜"	2¾"	3"	M	1
G	⅜"	2¹³⁄₁₆"	1¾"	M	1
H	⅜"	3¾"	6½"	M	1
I	⅜"	1½"	1¾"	M	1
J	⅛"	⅜"	4"	W	2
K	⅛"	⅜"	2¼"	W	2
L	⅜"	½"	⅝"	W	2

Bill of Materials

Material Key: W—walnut, M—maple
Supplies: 1—⅝X1¾" polished brass hinge hasp, 4—⅜" birch button plugs, 1 small padlock to fit hasp, rub-on letters or paint, adhesive-backed paper, finish.

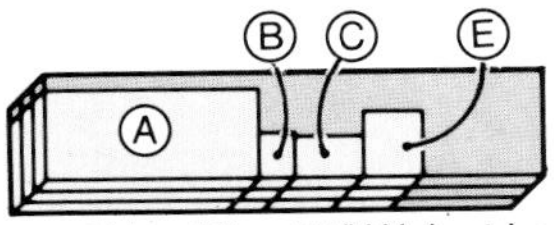
Ⓑ Ⓒ Ⓔ
Ⓐ

Cutting Diagram

1—2¼ × 5½ × 24" Walnut Lamination

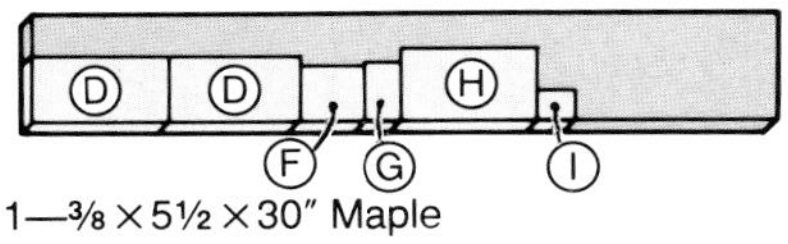
Ⓓ Ⓓ Ⓗ
Ⓕ Ⓖ Ⓘ

1—⅜ × 5½ × 30" Maple

cardboard. (We used the back of a writing tablet.) Tape the strips to the door edges. Now, insert the door in the rear opening to space the sides. Test-assemble and clamp. Check the sides and hood for square. Finally, glue and clamp the hood and sides to the chassis.

5. For the windshield (G), crosscut a 2"-long piece from the ⅜" maple. Next, bevel-rip one end as shown in the Section View on the Exploded View drawing *above*. Crosscut the piece 1¾" long, and rip it to fit the opening. Sand the opposite end to fit the back of the hood. Finish-sand, glue, and clamp it into place.

6. Crosscut a 7"-long piece from the ⅜" maple for the roof (H). From

continued

ARMORED-CAR BANK
continued

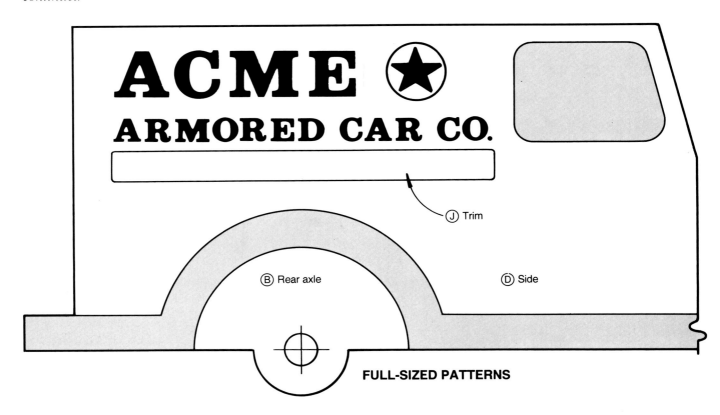

FULL-SIZED PATTERNS

it, rip one 1¹⁵⁄₁₆"-wide piece and one 1¹³⁄₁₆"-wide piece. Cut a ⅛x1⅛" coin slot from the edge of the wider piece where shown on the Roof Drawing *below.* (We cut in ⅛" with a bandsaw, and chiseled out the wood between the cuts.) Glue and clamp the two pieces edge to edge. Next, bevel-crosscut both ends of the roof, cutting it to 6½" finished length. Bevel the sides, and round over the top edges with sandpaper. Finally, finish-sand the roof and glue it to the car body.

7. To make the roof vent (I), rip from the remaining ⅜" maple, one piece ¹³⁄₁₆" wide, and one piece ¹¹⁄₁₆" wide. Crosscut both to 2" long. Cut the ⅛x1⅛" coin slot in the wider piece as shown on the Vent drawing *below.* Next, glue and clamp the two pieces together. Cut a bevel along the front edge, saw it to length, and round-over the back edge. Finish-sand the piece, and glue it to the roof.

Now, apply the trim

1. To make the trim strips, resaw a ¾x1x16" piece of walnut to ⅜" thickness. Rip one ⅛"-wide strip from the piece, and sand it. From that piece, crosscut two side strips (J), and two grill strips (K).

2. Glue the 4" walnut strips to both sides of the car. (We used masking tape to temporarily hold the strips.)

3. Mark the location of the four headlights on the front, using the dimensions in the Front View on the Exploded View drawing on *page 83.* Drill four ⅜" holes, ⁵⁄₁₆" deep. Glue a ⅜" button plug in each hole. Glue on the two trim pieces (K).

4. Cut the two walnut bumper pieces (L) to the size listed on the Bill of Materials. Glue them to the rear door where shown on the Door detail *opposite.*

5. Stain the wheels. (See the Buying Guide for a source of wheels and pegs.) Cut the toy axle

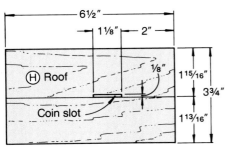

ROOF

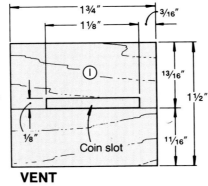

VENT

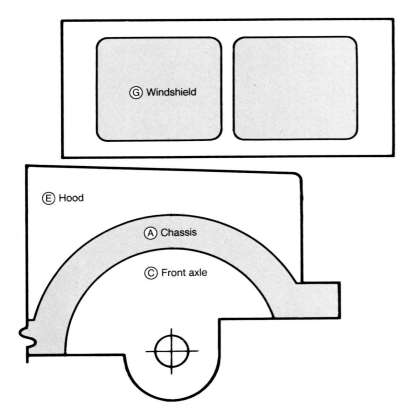

(G) Windshield

(E) Hood

(A) Chassis

(C) Front axle

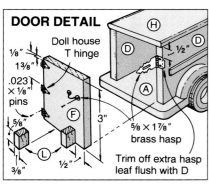

DOOR DETAIL

Doll house
T hinge

1/8"

1 3/8"

.023"
× 1/8"
pins

(H)

(D)   (D)

1/2"

(A)

5/8"

(F)   3"

(L)

3/8"   1/2"

5/8 × 1 7/8"
brass hasp

Trim off extra hasp
leaf flush with D

hinges to the door, and then to the side wall. (See the Buying Guide for a source of hinges and pins.) Finally, glue and nail the hasp (available at most hardware stores) in position. (We trimmed the end of the hasp flush with the side by sanding it on a stationary belt sander before attaching it to the car side.)

8. Paint or stencil the name of your choice on the car sides. (We used dry-transfer rub-on letters— 48 pt. Clarendon Bold for the large letters, and 24 pt. for the small letters—available at most art supply stores.)

9. Apply the finish of your choice. (We sprayed on three coats of semigloss polyurethane.)

Buying Guide

• **Armored Car Wheel and Hinge Package.** Includes two 2" single wheels with tread, two 2" dual wheels with tread, four toy axle pegs, three doll house T hinges, and one package of escutcheon pins. Catalog no. 8315. For current prices contact Meisel Hardware Specialties, P.O. Box 70, Mound, MN 55364. Phone: 612-471-8550.

Project Tool List
Tablesaw
Bandsaw
Disc/belt sander
Router
    1/4" round-over bit
Portable drill
    Bits: 11/32", 3/8"
    Doweling jig
Finishing sander

Note: We built the project using the tools listed. You may be able to substitute other tools or equipment for listed items you don't have. Additional common hand tools and clamps may be required to complete the project.

pegs to the length specified on the Exploded View drawing. Now, place the axle pegs through the wheels, and glue them in the axle holes.

6. Paint or stain the windows. (We traced the window patterns onto adhesive-backed paper [the pattern has to be flipped for the left side window], and then cut out the window silhouettes. We adhered the masks in position, and, as

shown *above*, stained the wood exposed in the mask cutouts using a cotton ball. We found a sparing amount of stain on the cotton ball worked best to keep the stain from running under the masks. Remove the masks immediately after staining.)

7. Using the dimensions on the Door Detail, glue (we used 5-minute epoxy) and nail the hasp eye, and the three doll house

LAMINATED PUZZLE BLOCK

7. Remove the patterns and tape from the block and block pieces. Remove the parts from the block and sand all sharp edges and cut surfaces on the pieces smooth.

Readying for display

1. If you wish to display the puzzle pieces above the block as we do in the photo *below*, drill seven ¼" holes in the top of the block where shown in the drawing *opposite, bottom* (draw diagonals from corner to corner to locate the center hole).

2. Cut the ¼" dowels to the lengths and quantity specified in the Supplies listing. Sand a slight taper on the ends of each dowel for easy insertion into the holes in the top of the block.

3. Position a ¼" dowel in each of the ¼" holes in the top of the block. Place the longest dowel in the center; the rest can be arranged in any order you wish.

Test your family's and friends' ingenuity again and again with this laminated puzzle block. And when displayed you'll also have an unusual conversation piece to admire.

Making and cutting the lamination

1. Cut two ¾" oak pieces (A), two ¾" walnut pieces (B), and one ½" cherry piece (C) to the sizes listed in the Bill of Materials *opposite*. (You can use other scraps you have at hand to form the lamination.)

2. Glue and clamp the pieces together in the configuration shown in the Bandsaw pattern *opposite* keeping the edges flush.

3. Scrape off any excess glue, and sand the block smooth. Also, sand a slight round-over on all edges.

4. Using carbon paper, transfer the full-sized Bandsaw pattern onto *two* pieces of paper measuring 3½×4" each. Apply spray adhesive to the back of the paper patterns and stick them onto two *adjoining* sides of the laminated block.

5. Drill a ¼" hole where shown on the pattern. Drill completely through the block, backing with stock to prevent chip-out. Turn the block to the other pattern, and drill the second ¼" hole completely through the block. (These holes provide a turn-around point for the bandsaw blade when cutting the patterns in the next step.)

6. Using a ⅛" blade, bandsaw the pattern on one side of the block. Now, tape the block so the cut parts remain in position in the block. Then, rotate the block and cut the second pattern.

Keep the puzzle pieces in the block as shown *above left,* or display them on dowels as shown *above*.

4. Drill a ¼" hole ⅜" deep in each puzzle piece for mounting on the dowels. (One at a time, we would hold a block piece on top of a dowel and decide on the best position to drill the hole. Also, drill these holes only on the surfaces cut with the bandsaw so they will not be visible when you assemble the block.)

5. Finish as desired. (We applied two coats of spray-on polyurethane varnish. The aerosol applicator makes it easier to cover all surfaces of the odd-shaped parts.)

Now, Can You Solve the Puzzle?

Test your ingenuity by putting all the pieces back into the block. (To figure out how the pieces went back together, we first assembled the block without the two small pieces. Once that was figured out, we removed all the pieces from the block, added the two small pieces, and reassembled the block. (Actually, it is much easier to reassemble the block and pieces than to describe.)

Project Tool List
Tablesaw
Bandsaw
Drill press
 ¼" bit
Finishing sander

Note: *We built the project using the tools listed. You may be able to substitute other tools or equipment for listed items you don't have. Additional common hand tools and clamps may be required to complete the project.*

BANDSAW PATTERN (Full Size)

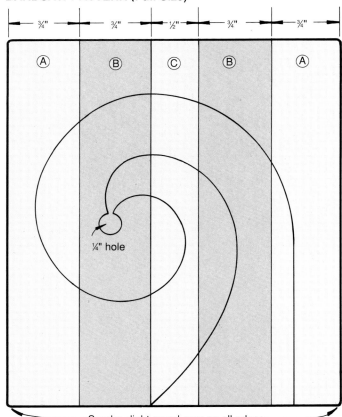

¼" hole

Sand a slight round-over on all edges.

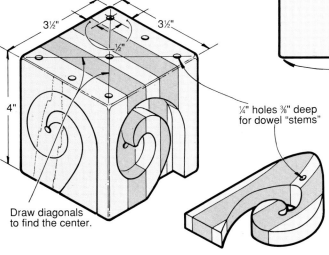

3½"   3½"
½"
4"

¼" holes ⅜" deep for dowel "stems"

Draw diagonals to find the center.

Bill of Materials					
Part	**Finished Size**			**Mat.**	**Qty.**
	T	**W**	**L**		
A	¾"	3½"	4"	O	2
B	¾"	3½"	4"	W	2
C	½"	3½"	4"	C	1

Material Key: O—oak, **W**—walnut, **C**—cherry
Supplies: Paper for pattern, carbon paper, spray adhesive, finish, ¼" dowel stems: one each at 2½", 6", and 7", two each at 3½" and 5"

UNITED STATES PUZZLE

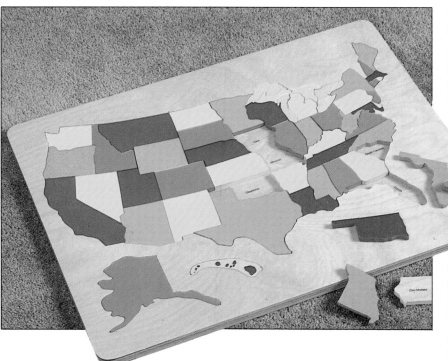

What's the capital city of Vermont? Can you identify the shape of Utah? If not, here's your chance to become a geography expert, help some favorite youngster become one, and have a lot of fun doing it. But before beginning the project, consider ordering the inexpensive stick-on U.S. map decals (state and capital names) from our Buying Guide source.

Note: Using the puzzle pattern on pages 90–91 and the cutting sequence indicated, we cut out our puzzle on a benchtop scrollsaw with a 16" throat. If your scrollsaw's throat measures less than 16", you may need to drill more start holes than we did, and cut out smaller sections of the continental United States before cutting the sections into individual states

First, make the puzzle parts

1. Cut two pieces of ⅜"-thick birch plywood to 17x22", one to serve as the puzzle top (A), the second one for the bottom (B). Now, set the bottom aside.

2. Increase the size of the map pattern on *pages 90–91* to 200 percent on an enlarging-type photocopying machine. (You will have to copy separate areas of the pattern, and then align and tape these copies together to form a complete pattern.) Trim the pattern along the borders, and then spray adhesive onto the back of the pattern. Now, align the pattern with the edges of the puzzle top (A), and adhere it.

3. Chuck a ¹⁄₁₆" drill bit in your drill press, and bore the eight blade start holes where indicated on the pattern. (We backed the puzzle top piece with scrap while drilling to prevent chip-out.)

4. Using a scrollsaw and a fine blade (ours had 20 teeth/inch), insert one end of the blade through blade start hole #1 in the puzzle top, and reattach it to the blade clamp. Turn on the saw and cut in

the direction indicated on the pattern for cut #1, where shown *below*. When you reach Texas, turn off the saw and carefully back the blade to start hole #1. Next, make cut #2 along the northern border to Lake Superior, and then along the Mississippi River to the point of Texas.

5. Remove the blade from the kerf and insert it through blade start hole #2. Reattach the blade, and then make cuts #3 and #4. Doing this allows you to lift out the large section of western states. Continue scrollsawing in this fashion until the lakes and eastern states section, Alaska, and the Hawaiian Islands are cut out. Now, cut the individual states to shape.

6. Cut two scrap pieces of ¾"-thick plywood or particleboard to 16½x21½". Brush a thin, even coat of yellow woodworker's glue onto the underside of the puzzle top. Now, place the puzzle top on the puzzle bottom and align the edges. Sandwich this lamination beween the scrap pieces, and clamp as shown *opposite*. Remove the adhered pattern from the puzzle top and all pieces. (We used lacquer thinner to dissolve the adhesive.)

7. After the glue dries, remove your clamps and scrap pieces from the lamination. Next, sand ⅜" radii on the corners following the dotted

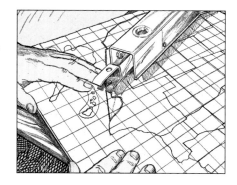

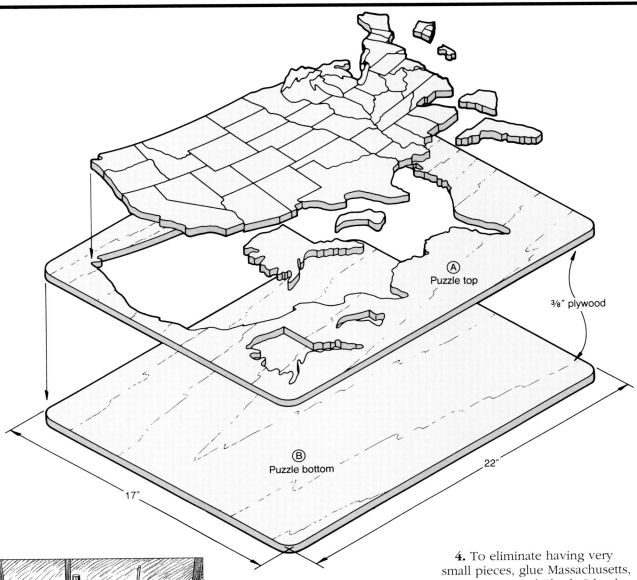

A. Puzzle top

3/8" plywood

B. Puzzle bottom

22"

17"

lines on the pattern. (We used a disc sander.) Hand- or belt-sand the remaining edges, removing all unevenness and glue squeeze-out.

Now, finish the puzzle

1. Finish-sand the lamination with fine sandpaper (we used 220 grit). Wipe off the dust and set the pieces on a clean surface, top side up.

2. Spray a coat of clear lacquer on the pieces and lamination to seal the wood for painting. Let dry, and then turn the pieces over and spray the bottoms. Again, lightly sand the pieces smooth with fine sandpaper.

3. Paint the edges and tops of each state and lake piece. Use our color key on *page 91* and follow the numbers on the pattern, or use your own color scheme. (We applied two coats of spray enamel paint to each puzzle piece.) Sand any paint from the bottom surface of the pieces.

4. To eliminate having very small pieces, glue Massachusetts, Connecticut, and Rhode Island together. (We used quick-setting epoxy but other glues will also work.) Glue the Maryland and Delaware pieces together for the same reason.

5. Now, spray a final coat of clear finish (we used semigloss lacquer) over the entire lamination. Let dry.

6. Place the puzzle pieces in the lamination's recesses. Now, working with one state at a time, cut out the stick-on decals for that state. Peel off the backing and apply the state decal to the top face, of the lamination's bottom. Next, apply the capital city decal to the underside of each state as
continued

UNITED STATES PUZZLE
continued

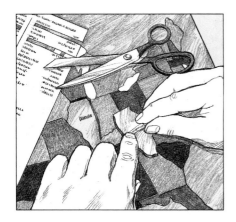

shown *above*. Press the decal onto the wood, and burnish it for a strong bond. Finish applying all of the decals and you'll soon be ready for your first geography quiz.

Buying Guide
• **Stick-on U.S. map decals.**
Order #8901—states, capital cities, and lakes decals. For current price, contact Meisel Hardware Specialties, P.O. Box 70, Mound, MN 55364.

Supplies
Five colors of nontoxic paint; polyurethane finish.

Project Tool List
Tablesaw
Scrollsaw
Disc sander
Drill press
  ⅟₁₆" bit
Finishing sander

Note: We built the project using the tools listed. You may be able to substitute other tools or equipment for listed items you don't have. Additional common hand tools and clamps may be required to complete the project.

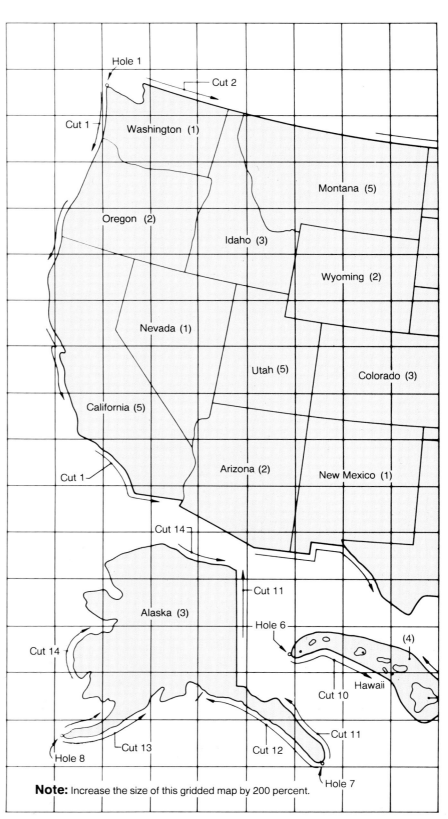

Hole 1
Cut 2
Cut 1
Washington (1)
Montana (5)
Oregon (2)
Idaho (3)
Wyoming (2)
Nevada (1)
Utah (5)
Colorado (3)
California (5)
Arizona (2)
New Mexico (1)
Cut 14
Cut 11
Alaska (3)
Hole 6
(4)
Cut 14
Hawaii
Cut 10
Hole 8
Cut 13
Cut 12
Cut 11
Hole 7

Note: Increase the size of this gridded map by 200 percent.

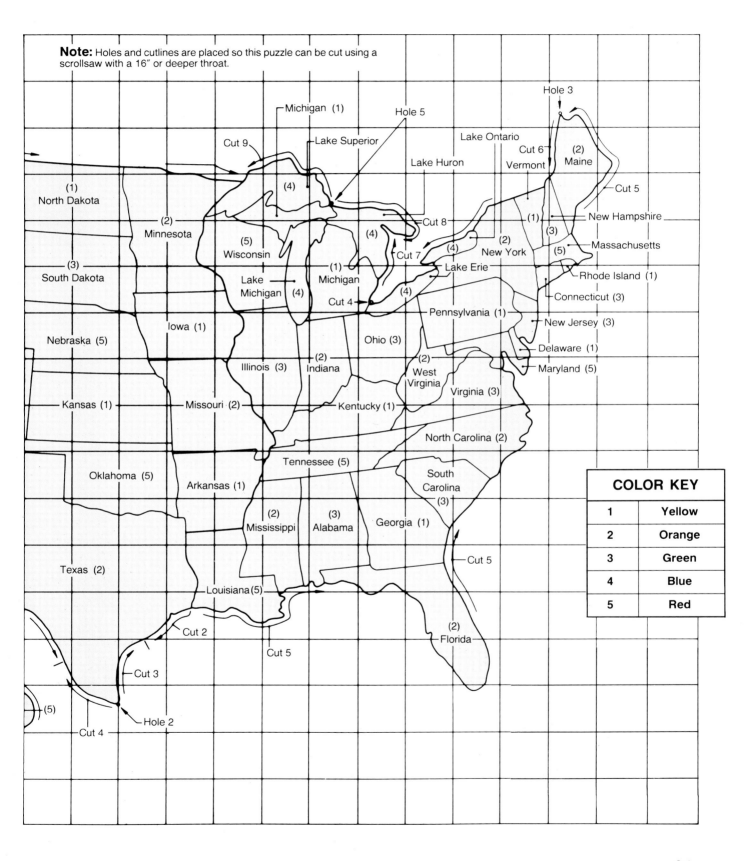

Note: Holes and cutlines are placed so this puzzle can be cut using a scrollsaw with a 16″ or deeper throat.

Michigan (1)

Hole 5

Hole 3

Lake Ontario

Cut 9

Lake Superior

Lake Huron

Cut 6

Vermont

(2)
Maine

(1)
North Dakota

(4)

Cut 5

(2)
Minnesota

Cut 8

(1)
New Hampshire

(5)
Wisconsin

(4)

(4)

(3)

Massachusetts

Cut 7

(4)

(2)
New York

(5)

(3)
South Dakota

(1)
Michigan

Cut 4

Lake
Michigan

(4)

Lake Erie

Rhode Island (1)

Connecticut (3)

(4)

Pennsylvania (1)

New Jersey (3)

Iowa (1)

Ohio (3)

Delaware (1)

Nebraska (5)

(2)
Indiana

(2)
West
Virginia

Maryland (5)

Illinois (3)

Virginia (3)

Kansas (1)

Missouri (2)

Kentucky (1)

North Carolina (2)

Tennessee (5)

Oklahoma (5)

South
Carolina
(3)

Arkansas (1)

(2)
Mississippi

(3)
Alabama

Georgia (1)

Texas (2)

Cut 5

Louisiana (5)

Cut 2

(2)
Florida

Cut 5

Cut 3

(5)

Hole 2

Cut 4

COLOR KEY	
1	Yellow
2	Orange
3	Green
4	Blue
5	Red

ACROBATIC CLOWN

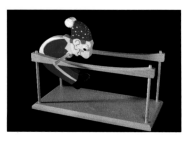

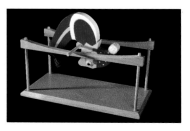

It's not really a perpetual-motion machine, but once launched, our rolling clown will spin and change directions on the parallel bars several times. Kids of all ages can't resist watching it.

Note: We cut all the parts from a ¾x5½x24" piece of clear pine. To do this, we first cut out the clown, and then planed the remaining board to ½" thickness. (See the Cutting Diagram below.)

Let's start with the clown cutout

1. Transfer the full-sized pattern of the clown (A), shown *opposite,* onto a ¾"-thick piece of clear pine. (We used carbon paper.) Include the detail lines for the clothing, hands, face, and the location of the ¼" hole. Next, using a scrollsaw or bandsaw, saw the clown to shape.

2. Chuck a ¼" brad-point bit in your drill press, and drill the hole through the clown's hand. (We placed a piece of scrap under the workpiece to prevent chip-out.)

3. To transfer the pattern to the clown's second side, make another copy of the pattern and tape it to a window, pattern-side against the glass. Now, relying on daylight to make the pattern visible through the paper, trace over the clown pattern lines with a pencil as shown at *right.* (This creates a *reversed* pattern.) Remove the copy from the window, place the reversed pattern on carbon paper, and cut around it. Next, tape it and the carbon paper to the unmarked side of the clown cutout, aligning all edges. Now, trace the pattern onto the cutout. Remove the pattern and carbon paper; then set the clown aside.

Now, make the parallel bars and base

1. If you start as we did, with a ¾ x5½x24" board, plane the remaining piece to ½"-thick. (Or purchase a piece of ½" pine.) Next, cut out the base (B), using the dimensions on the Bill Of Materials.

2. Chuck a chamfer bit in your router, and rout a ¼" chamfer along the top edges of the base where shown on the Exploded View drawing *below right.* (We used a tablemounted router.)

Bill of Materials

Part	Finished Size*			Mat.	Qty.
	T	W	L		
A clown	¾"	5½"	6½"	P	1
B base	½"	5"	10¼"	P	1
C bar	½"	¾"	10"	P	2

Material Key: P—pine
Supplies: Acrylic paints (6 colors), ¼" dowel.

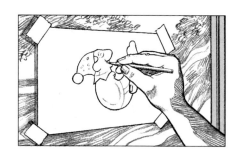

3. Rip the remaining piece of ½" stock to create two equal halves. Using double-faced tape, stick the pieces together, aligning the edges and ends. Make a full-sized pattern of the parallel bar (C), *opposite,* and trace it onto the face of one piece, aligning the bottom with the straight edge of the wood. (A photocopy of the pattern adhered to the wood with spray adhesive also works well.) Saw the parallel

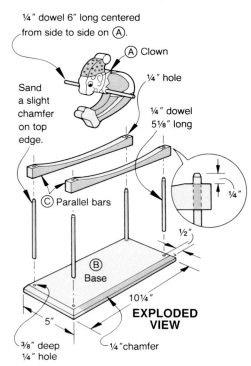

¼" dowel 6" long centered from side to side on (A).

(A) Clown

¼" hole

Sand a slight chamfer on top edge.

¼" dowel 5⅛" long

(C) Parallel bars

¼"

½"

(B) Base

10¼"

5"

EXPLODED VIEW

⅜" deep ¼" hole

¼" chamfer

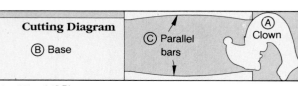

Cutting Diagram

(B) Base

(C) Parallel bars

(A) Clown

¾ × 5½ × 24" Pine

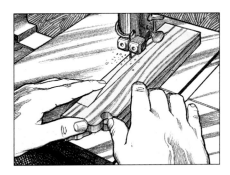

bars (See *above*.) Lightly sand the curved surfaces of the pieces (we used a drum sander). Separate the pieces. Now, finish-sand all parts.

4. Chuck a ¼" bit in your drill press. Clamp a fence on the table ¼" away from the center of the bit. Next, place a mark ⅜" in from the ends on the top edge of each bar. Back the workpiece with scrap and drill the ¼" holes through the pieces. (See the detail on the Exploded View drawing.)

5. Move the fence ½" away from the center of the drill bit. Adjust your drill press so the bit extends to ⅜" from the tabletop. Mark the centerpoints for the four ¼" holes ½" in from each corner on the base. Drill the holes.

6. Cut four pieces of ¼" dowel to 5⅛" long and one to 6" long. Sand a slight chamfer on one end of the four short dowels.

Assemble the project and supply the finish

1. Apply glue to the unchamfered ends of the 5⅛"-long dowels and insert them into the holes in the base. (We used yellow woodworker's glue.) Apply glue in the holes in the parallel bars and slip them onto the chamfered ends of the dowels, and push down until ¼" of the dowels protrudes. Finally, apply glue in the hole in the clown, insert the 6"-long dowel through the hole, and then center the clown on it.

2. Finish the project. (We applied two coats of spray varnish to the parallel bars and base, and one coat to the clown to serve as a wood sealer. Then,

we lightly sanded the top surface of the parallel bars crosswise with 80-grit sandpaper to improve traction for the clown when rolling up the bar's incline. Following the transferred lines on the clown, we then painted it with acrylic paints. See the pattern for our color selections.) Apply a finish coat of varnish to the clown. Add the adhesive-backed toy eyes, or paint the eyes on. (See the Buying Guide for our source of eyes.)

Buying Guide
• **Toy animal eyes.**
⁷⁄₁₆" diameter, catalog no. ME-3. For current price, contact Armor Products, Box 445, East Northport, NY 11731. Phone 516-462-6228.

Project Tool List
Tablesaw
Bandsaw or scrollsaw
Drill press
  ¼" bit
  Drum sander
Router
  Router table
  Chamfer bit
Finishing sander

Note: *We built the project using the tools listed. You may be able to substitute other tools or equipment for listed items you don't have. Additional common hand tools and clamps may be required to complete the project.*

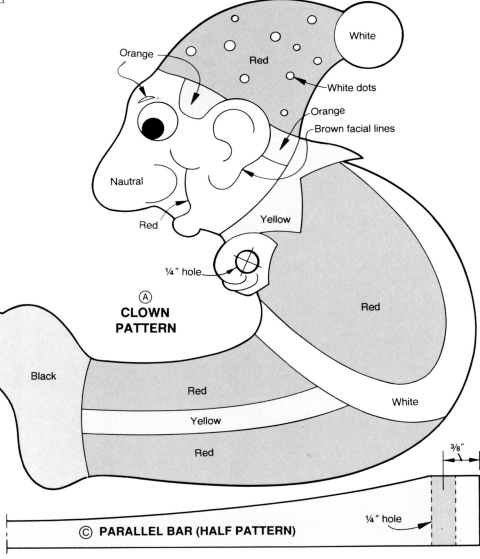

LURE-OF-THE-SEA RELIEF PUZZLE

When you scrollsaw and paint the parts for this colorful coastal scene, you're setting sail for a good time. Place the puzzle in a child's longing hands or on a shelf for its pure visual beauty.

1. Cut a ¾" clear pine board to 7×11". Sand the front and back of the board. Transfer the full-sized pattern to the stock, aligning the bottom of the pattern with the bottom of the board. (We made a photocopy of the pattern and mounted it to the stock with spray-on adhesive.)

2. Scrollsaw around the outside of the frame. (Using a #9 blade, we sawed just outside the cutline.) Drill a ³⁄₃₂" blade start hole through the board where marked on the pattern and thread the scrollsaw blade through the hole. Cut the interior edge of the frame. Switch to a #6 blade and cut the individual pieces to shape. Remove the paper pattern pieces. (We used lacquer thinner to dissolve the adhesive.)

3. Lay the pine frame on a piece of ⅛"-thick plywood or hardboard,

and trace the frame's outline on it. Cut the backing to shape. With the edges flush, glue the backing to the frame. Sand flush the edges of frame and backing.

4. To create the three-dimensional effect, sand the sky and sun pieces to reduce the thickness to ½". (We used a stationary sander; a belt sander also would work.) Finish-sand all the pieces.

5. Finally, following the lead of the photo *above* or your own imagination, paint or dye the puzzle pieces. For an easier-to-assemble puzzle, paint just the front and side surfaces. To make assembling the puzzle more challenging, paint all surfaces of the pieces.

(We used wood dyes for the colored pieces; watered-down acrylic paints also work well. We left the sail pieces, frame, and parts of the lighthouse natural. Later, we applied several coats of mineral oil to all the pieces to seal them.)

Project Tool List
Tablesaw
Scrollsaw
Drill press
³⁄₃₂" bit
Disc/belt sander
Finishing sander

Note: *We built the project using the tools listed. You may be able to substitute other tools or equipment for listed items you don't have. Additional common hand tools and clamps may be required to complete the project.*

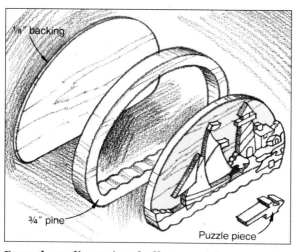

⅛" backing
¾" pine
Puzzle piece

For a three-dimensional effect, sand the sun and sky pieces to ½" thick (light-gray area).

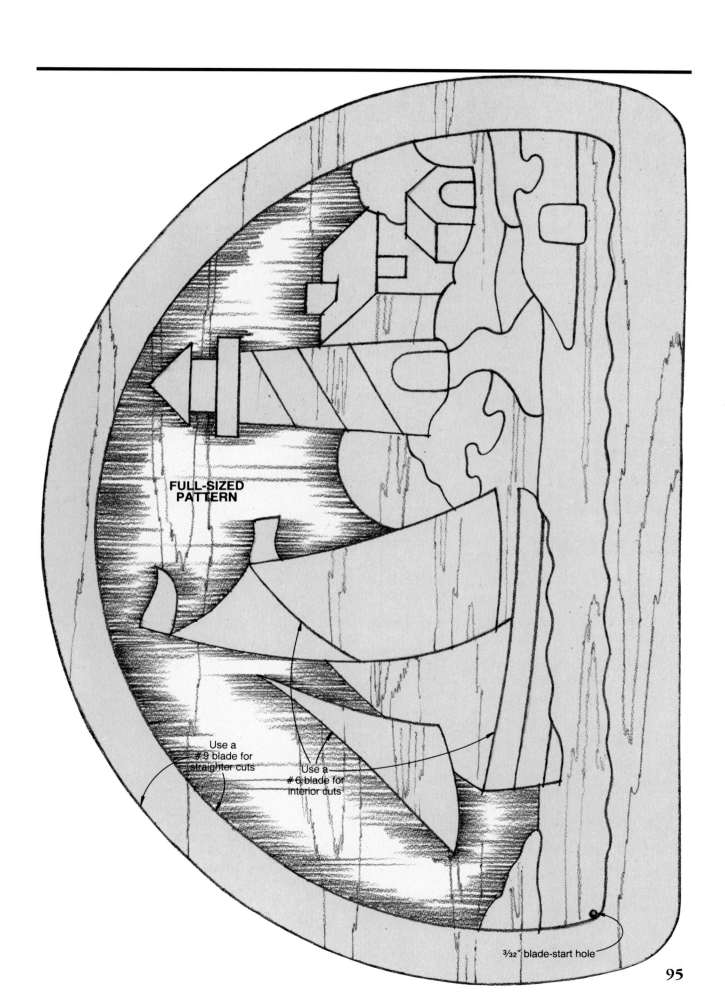

FULL-SIZED PATTERN

Use a
9 blade for
straighter cuts

Use a
6 blade for
interior cuts

³/₃₂″ blade-start hole

ACKNOWLEDGMENTS

Project Designers

Dave Ashe—A Kid's Retreat, pages 18–22; Lamp-Ness Creature, pages 52–55

Jim Boelling—Night-Light Clown, pages 31–33

Sherry Connors—Toy Display Shelf, pages 44–45

John Cooper—Armored-Car Bank, pages 82–85

Scott B. Darragh—Wagons, Ho!, pages 11–15

David Donnelly—Ferris Wheel, pages 65–67

James R. Downing—Kids' Play Structure, pages 5–10; Armored-Car Bank, pages 82–85

Jamie Downing—A Young Skipper's Stool, pages 60–63

Kim Downing—Wall-Hung Game Cabinet, pages 38–41

Richard Gard—Teddy Bear Music Box, pages 72–75

Harlequin Crafts—Ark-ed Doorway, pages 34–37; An Aquatic Clothes Tree for Youngsters, pages 42–43

Michael G. Harrington—pattern for Fun-Time Tote Box, page 80

Don Hart—High-Flying Balloon Mobile, pages 46–49

Susan Henry—painting for Fun-Time Tote Box, page 81

Al Horowitz—Alpine-Ride Action Toy, pages 68–71

Marlen Kemmet—Big-Hit Baseball Bat, pages 26–27

George Myhervold—Big-League Organizer, pages 23–25; Safari Shelves, pages 56–59; Alpine-Ride Action Toy, pages 68–71

The Puzzle People—United States Puzzle, pages 88–91

Russell Greenslade Designs—Lure-of-the-Sea Relief Puzzle, pages 94–95

Gene Scherer—Dinosaur Mirror, pages 50–51

Bob Sellers—Pint-Sized Picnic Table, pages 28–29

Bill and Poly See—Acrobatic Clown, pages 92–93

Chet Snouffer—Build Your Own Boomerang, pages 16–17

Tom Lewis Wooden Toys—One Lean Jelly Bean Machine, pages 76–78

James B. Woodruff—Laminated Puzzle Block, pages 86–87

Photographers

Bob Calmer
Jim Elder
John Hetherington
Bill Hopkins
Hopkins Associates
Jim Kascoutas
Perry Struse

Illustrators

Jamie Downing
Kim Downing
Lippisch Design Inc.
Carson Ode
Ode Designs
Greg Roberts
Jim Stevenson
Bill Zaun

If you would like to order any additional copies of our books, call 1-800-678-2802 or check with your local bookstore.